Evidence of What Is Said

Ann Charters | Charles Olson

Evidence of What Is Said

The Correspondence between
Ann Charters and Charles Olson
about History and Herman Melville

with an Introductory Essay and Photographs
of Olson in Gloucester by Ann Charters

TAVERN BOOKS

PORTLAND

Cover: facsimile of a Charles Olson letter.

The letters and postcards comprising the correspondence between
Ann Charters and Charles Olson are deposited in the Charles Olson
Archive in the Special Collections of the Thomas J. Dodd Research
Center at the University of Connecticut in Storrs, CT.

Charles Olson, 1910-1970
Ann Charters, 1936-

ISBN-13: 978-1-935635-50-5 (paperback)
ISBN-13: 978-1-935635-51-2 (hardcover)

LCCN: 2015936519

FIRST EDITION

98765432 First Printing

TAVERN BOOKS
Union Station
800 NW 6th Avenue #255
Portland, Oregon 97209
www.tavernbooks.org

Introduction

I would be an historian as Herodotus was, looking
for oneself for the evidence of
what is said. . . .

Charles Olson, from "Letter 23" in *The Maximus Poems*

Early on the winter morning of January 7, 1968, I sat down at my
Olivetti portable typewriter in Brooklyn Heights, New York, to write
my first letter to the poet Charles Olson at 28 Fort Square, Gloucester,
Massachusetts. I wanted to tell him that I was embarking upon a study
of his book about Herman Melville, *Call Me Ishmael* (1947). The
California publisher Robert Hawley, who had been Olson's student at
Black Mountain College, suggested that I write such a book for his small
press Oyez in Berkeley. At Black Mountain, Olson had encouraged
Hawley to pursue his interest in the subject of Western Americana and
helped him to begin his career as a bookseller by giving him the task of
cataloging the books in the library before the college closed down in the
spring of 1956.

Recently Hawley had met my husband Sam in Berkeley, who
told him that I had written a chapter on Melville for my dissertation
at Columbia University in 1965. Hawley's small press specialized

in beautifully printed poetry broadsides and books by his favorite California poets, a list that included Brother Antoninus (William Everson), Robert Duncan, Philip Lamantia, Mary Fabilli, Lew Welch, Josephine Miles, and David Meltzer, among others. When Sam passed on Hawley's invitation, I didn't believe him, so I wrote and asked Hawley if he were serious. Robert answered immediately: "Was most sincere—clear-eyed & aware—about Olson essay. Will look forward to reading whatever you decide to write."

I didn't know much about Charles Olson. I had originally encountered his poetry in the pages of little magazines such as *Contact, Black Mountain Review, Origin,* and *Ark/Moby* that sprouted like mushrooms in the 1950s. In 1956-57 Sam had introduced me to small press publications at the City Lights Bookshop in San Francisco. Then I was an impecunious undergraduate English major at the University of California at Berkeley, and I couldn't afford to buy any of them. I hadn't owned any examples of Olson's writing until a few years later, after I had moved to New York City, where I bought Donald Allen's ground-breaking anthology *The New American Poetry 1945-1960.*

I thought that Olson's essay "Projective Verse" was the most substantial statement of aesthetics in the concluding section of that book, and I was impressed by the scope and power of Olson's vision in the selection of his poetry at the beginning of the anthology, especially his Maximus poems. These were part of a series of poems, songs, and letters addressed over the years by his persona, the poet/philosopher Maximus, to his beloved harbor town of Gloucester, Massachusetts. Olson had created them in much the same spirit that William Carlos Williams was writing his post-Poundian epic *Paterson* about his New

Jersey city. I admired Williams' poetry, and I was intrigued by what I had read of Olson's work, so my instinct told me to accept Hawley's offer.

Actually I was drawn to Olson by something I read on page 13 of *The New American Poetry*, a few lines in the middle of one of the early "Songs of Maximus."

> Holes
> in my shoes, that's all right, my fly
> gaping, me out
> at the elbows, the blessing
> that difficulties are once more
> "In the midst of plenty, walk
> as close to
> bare
> In the face of sweetness,
>
> piss
>
> In the time of goodness,
> go side, go
> smashing, beat them, go as
> (as near as you can
>
> tear
>
> In the land of plenty, have

nothing to do with it
          take the way of
the lowest,
including your legs, go
contrary, go

sing

I was caught by the mixture of spontaneity and toughness in Olson's voice. In his confident assertion of his nonconformity I caught echoes of the tradition of his spiritual ancestors, the New England Transcendentalists Ralph Waldo Emerson and Henry David Thoreau. I also took these lines personally. I had heard that Olson was a great teacher and an important influence on many younger poets. As I read these words and other Maximus poems in the anthology over and over again, they seemed to encourage the potential for creativity within me, even before I sensed it for myself.

When I began to study Olson's involvement with Melville, I learned from Olson's bibliography that *Call Me Ishmael: A Study of Melville* had been his first book, published by Reynal and Hitchcock in New York City in 1947, a few years before he began writing Maximus poems. It didn't attract much attention in the United States, but a French translation had been published by the major press Gallimard in Paris and a Swedish translation was published later by the small press Janus in Sollentuna. Olson told me that in 1946, when he had shown the manuscript of his book to Ezra Pound in St. Elizabeth's Hospital, Pound had suggested he send a copy to T.S. Eliot, who was influential at Faber & Faber publishers in London. Pound wrote Eliot that Olson's study was so good that it would save Eliot the trouble of ever having to read Melville's novel. Eliot apparently loathed *Moby-Dick*, and he turned down Olson's manuscript.

Twenty years later, *Call Me Ishmael* was published in London in 1967 as a Cape Edition by Jonathan Cape. It was on a distinguished list with Claude Lévi-Strauss's *The Memorandum,* José Ortega y Gasset's *On Love: Aspects of a Single Theme,* and William Carlos Williams's *I Wanted to Write a Poem.* I bought the Cape Edition of *Call Me Ishmael* at the Gotham Book Mart in midtown Manhattan, but the book's margins were too narrow for me to write on. Robert Wilson, the owner of the Phoenix Bookshop in Greenwich Village who had asked me to compile a Jack Kerouac bibliography, helped me to hunt down a rare copy of the first American cloth-bound edition of Olson's book. I couldn't bring myself to make notes on its pages, so for my study I used an inexpensive reprint of the Reynal and Hitchcock edition conveniently issued in paperback by Grove Evergreen shortly before I started on the project.

When I agreed to write the book for Hawley I made one condition: that he send me Olson's address so I could correspond with him if I had any questions about his interpretation of Melville. It is fair to say that I was as interested in Melville as I was in Olson at the beginning of my study. Once I began reading closely, I was fascinated by the originality and force of the literary style of *Call Me Ishmael.* Since Kerouac had helped me to compile his bibliography the previous year, I decided to write to Olson and invite him to participate in my work.

I sent off my first letter to him completely unaware of his earlier extensive correspondences with Frances Boldereff, Cid Corman, and Robert Creeley, among many others. Olson responded by return mail with his typical energy and enthusiasm. Later I learned that in January 8, 1968, the day after I wrote my first letter to him, he created a short Maximus poem about the winter scene outside his windows in Gloucester that reflected his high spirits:

The sea's
boiling   the land's
boiling   all the winds
of the earth are turning
the snow into sand—and
hiss, the land into
desert sands   the place
into hell.   snow wild
        snow and hissing
        waters

In mid-January I went to San Francisco with Sam and our six-month-old daughter Mallay for a Country Joe and the Fish concert, the acid-rock band Sam was producing for Vanguard Records. I met Hawley, who introduced me to Olson's associate at Black Mountain College, the poet Robert Duncan. Back home, I picked up my correspondence with Olson on February 1, 1968. From then on our letters flew back and forth between Brooklyn Heights and Gloucester, mine filled with questions about chronology and biographical background, his filled with oblique answers and tantalizing hints about things I knew nothing about. For example, he suggested that I could find books from Melville's library in a private collection in my neighborhood; then he refused to come forth with sufficient details for me to track them down. Olson could have been teasing me, but I regarded it as a trifling matter compared with the material he generously shared describing the composition of *Call Me Ishmael*.

By the middle of March 1968, I had organized my notes and begun writing about Olson and Melville. Mostly I worked nights, after I'd put my baby daughter to bed and finished grading student compositions and planning the English classes I taught at New York City Community College nearby. In April, during my spring break from the college, Sam and I drove to Gloucester on the chance that we might visit with Olson, but we found out that he was away in San Francisco at that time. Our first meeting had to be postponed until my summer break from teaching.

For the rest of the spring, I continued to work on the book. Finally on June 13, 1968, just before we celebrated Mallay's first birthday, I drove off to Gloucester to spend two days with Olson while Sam stayed home to keep our baby daughter company. By this time I considered *Olson/Melville: A Study in Affinity*, the title I'd given to my study, nearly finished. I had only two questions left to ask Olson, but I was curious to meet him and eager to take photographs of him and his Gloucester neighborhood to illustrate my book.

The morning I left Brooklyn Heights, driving our 1962 orange VW Beetle up to Gloucester, I remember being nervous because Olson was rumored to be so tall—almost a giant, Hawley had told me—and I was afraid he would physically intimidate me. I knew that ever since the death of his common-law wife Betty in an automobile accident in 1964, he had lived alone. He was supposed to be very thin-skinned about criticism of his work. I didn't know what I would say if he asked to see what I'd written about him, because I was not uncritical of his reading of Melville. I needn't have worried. Fortunately, while I was his houseguest Olson never asked what I'd written about him, so I was never forced into the role of Jack the Giant Killer. And I was about to see for myself that though Olson *was* tall, he wasn't a clumsy, intimidating storybook giant. At fifty-seven years old, he carried his six-foot, eight-inch height and corresponding bulk with considerable grace.

Just outside Boston I took the highway northeast to Cape Ann and then followed the turnoff onto the winding road that led to the seacoast town of Gloucester. Sam and I had already scouted the route previously on our April trip. In the crowded downtown center, I found the street leading to the waterfront and approached Fort Point, the section of town where Olson lived. He called it "the Fort." It was a small district of shabby wooden houses. The paved streets were filled with potholes. Decaying piers led to scattered fishing boats tied up in the harbor. Nearby, the Cape Ann Fisheries' wharf and a ramshackle cannery processing cat food and smelling strongly of fish were magnets for the raucous seagulls that congregated on the shifting air currents overhead.

I arrived at the Fort around noon, relieved to have finished the long drive. Finally, after the months I'd been thinking and writing about Olson, I was about to meet him. I parked my car on the street as close as I could come to his address. He had rented his apartment at 28 Fort Square Avenue for over a decade, ever since Black Mountain College had closed down. It was in a weathered two-story frame house painted a faded white and divided into four apartments. I climbed the few uneven cement steps up to the yard beside the house. A broken sidewalk led through a tangle of bushes around to the back, taking me past a load of laundry hanging on clotheslines and a blue-painted plaster statue of the Madonna in an overgrown patch of grass.

The path brought me to a flight of wooden steps at the back of the building. Clutching my camera bag to my side, I climbed up to where Olson had told me he lived in the second-floor apartment to the right of the stairs. A large wooden storm door was propped against the wall on the narrow porch. In April, Sam and I had peered through the glass in Olson's front door into his deserted kitchen. Now I saw two people inside, sitting together at the kitchen table, and when I knocked the taller man got up to open the door.

Olson stood before me framed in the doorway. He was dressed in a light-blue, un-ironed cotton short-sleeved dress shirt and a pair of baggy slacks. Obviously he hadn't been awake for very long. He was as tall as Hawley had described him, but I didn't find his size menacing. He had gray stubble on his plump cheeks, and behind his large glasses his blue eyes seemed kind, if a little puzzled to see me. He sized me up quickly, remembered who I was, and welcomed me inside. When he spoke, I noticed that his accent sounded less pronouncedly Massachusetts than Kerouac's, though both men had been born in cities—Lowell and Worcester—in the same state.

Stepping over the threshold, I noticed that the person still seated at the kitchen table was much younger than Olson, about my age. He hadn't bothered to comb his hair, and he wore a rumpled tee-shirt and a pair of chinos. His eyes looked tired behind his black-rimmed glasses, as if he had stayed up too late the night before. Olson introduced him as

George Butterick and told me that he'd been living for several weeks in the apartment next door. Butterick was helping Olson sort through his cartons of manuscripts, or as Olson described it to me, helping him with the herculean task of "catching up with 'paper.'" I knew that Butterick and Albert Glover, another graduate student who had taken Olson's seminars at the State University of New York at Buffalo, had compiled the bibliography of Olson's work that I used when I began my study of Olson's writing about Melville.

After Olson shut the rickety door behind me, he moved about the small kitchen quickly, clearing papers and books off a straight-backed chair near the door so I could join him and Butterick at the battered wooden table. He picked up a dented aluminum pot standing on a big range-style oil stove and poured coffee into a thick white cup left beside the sink. I watched him place the cup on the table in front of the empty chair and refill his own cup, all the while urging me to sit down. Back at the table, he scratched his balding head with his left hand. Then, with what I later realized was a habitual gesture, he shook out an oversized cigarette from the crumpled pack of Pall Malls he held in his right hand, lit it smoothly from the one still in his mouth, and stubbed out the old one in an overflowing ashtray. Even seated he was a large man. As his friend the poet Joel Oppenheimer later told me, "Charles held a Pall Mall like you or I hold the stub of a Camel." Pall Mall cigarettes were much longer than standard-size American cigarettes like Camels.

Apparently before my arrival, Butterick had told Olson that I was Kerouac's bibliographer, and both George and Charles immediately joined forces to bait me. Why did I care so much about Kerouac's books? What made me think his writing was worth my time? They made it clear that they thought Kerouac was an intellectual lightweight, a crowd-pleasing novelist beneath their consideration as a popular writer.

Later, Olson told me with great amusement that last February, Kerouac—who was then living in nearby Lowell—had made an unexpected pilgrimage to his doorstep in Gloucester to get drunk with him and celebrate the publication of *Vanity of Duluoz*, his latest "true life novel." As Jack was leaving, Charles impulsively lined the slushy steps of his back stairs with newspapers for his guest to step on, including pages from that day's *Boston Globe* containing a review of Kerouac's book. It was a theatrical gesture to show how little Olson thought of it. When I listened to Charles tell me this story, I sensed that it also revealed how much he chafed at his isolation during his long winters in Gloucester, and how much he would have welcomed some of the attention Kerouac was getting for his work.

During my years as a graduate student, I had lots of practice defending my interest in Kerouac to hostile listeners. After only a couple of minutes at Olson's kitchen table, I recognized a familiar atmosphere. It reminded me of many of the American Literature seminars I'd attended at Columbia. Now Olson was taking on the role of the older, experienced instructor siding with a favorite graduate student against a newcomer. When I answered their questions, I bantered with them in the spirit of a ritual academic hazing, and I began to feel a little less like an interloper.

I turned to Butterick to tell him how useful his Olson bibliography had been to me. As I spoke, I saw from the tense expression on George's face and his guarded reply that he probably didn't want to hear anything about what I'd written about Olson and Melville. Olson had chosen

Butterick, still working on his doctorate, to be the general editor of his papers, and George was reluctant to welcome a newcomer. His response to me was understandable, and it assuaged my second concern about the visit. Since the Olson/Butterick relationship had been established for several years, I *was* an interloper so far as George was concerned. Charles was close to George and understood how he must have felt about me. I realized that while I was with them, probably Olson would be too tactful to bring up the subject of my book. With great relief I understood that I wasn't going to have to defend my ideas about the Olson/Melville affinity to either of them. I took my camera bag off my lap, put it down on the scuffed kitchen floor, and settled back to drink my coffee while I looked around the apartment.

Olson's second-floor kitchen was at the rear of the house. His windows looked south out over the rooftops of the buildings across the street onto a bay where fishing boats and other small craft headed out to sea, a wide expanse of open water stretching from Eastern Point to Western Harbor. Flimsy white curtains and a dark shade blocked some of the expanse of the clear blue sky outdoors, but the windows helped to illuminate and open out the space inside the narrow apartment. The two rooms I could see were crowded with well-worn furniture that had probably come from a local Goodwill or Salvation Army store. Scattered piles of Olson's books and manuscripts were spread out everywhere. His books even overflowed onto the dark-brown painted wooden floor in the small room adjoining the kitchen that apparently served Olson as a study. I imagined that the apartment would feel claustrophobic, as well as cold and drafty, during Gloucester's long winters. Since the sole source of heat in the apartment was the kitchen stove, Olson rarely left its side. As he later confided to a friend, "Trouble is, my one spot really *is* this kitchen table."

On the door in the middle of the apartment, Olson had tacked a large charcoal sketch of tree trunks and three photographs of himself from his years at Black Mountain College. When I turned around, I saw that he had covered the kitchen wall next to my chair with an old, faded topological survey map of the Atlantic Ocean showing the Gloucester area that he described in his Maximus poems. Riddled with notes and scraps of paper where Olson had annotated significant places and dates, the map sagged with all the attention that he'd paid to it over the years he'd been writing his epic poem.

I began to feel at ease in Olson's physical presence, but what made me feel at home in his apartment was that I responded positively to his personal style. Nobody I'd ever met wore a pair of well-worn tennis shoes and a threadbare dress shirt so nonchalantly. Nobody I'd ever visited had lived in such a chaos of manuscripts and books, abandoned coffee cups, unwashed dishes, empty Cutty Sark scotch bottles and overflowing ashtrays. I'd never been in an apartment like it before, but I recognized it as the working environment of a dedicated poet so I felt right at home.

Once Olson started to talk, we sat at the kitchen table for several hours. At some point I got hungry, but I have only a dim memory of actually eating any lunch. We must have had bread and soup. Mostly I remember that Olson didn't have to get up from the table to prepare the soup. He just reached his long arm over to the stove and turned a knob. Then he struck a wooden match, held it to the burner, and heated up a large pot of marrow soup. It had been left there for him by Ronni

Goldfarb, another graduate student at Buffalo who also lived next door during the summer. She served as his housekeeper, coming in daily to cook and occasionally to clean his apartment.

That afternoon, Charles, George, and I never budged from the kitchen table while our talk went on and on. We consumed endless cups of coffee and, as the hours passed, quite a few shots of Cutty Sark. Late in the afternoon the weather turned chilly. Olson put on an old brown corduroy jacket and George disappeared briefly into his room next door to put on a shirt before we went outside for a walk. Olson had agreed to let me take photographs of him in his Gloucester neighborhood, and I was eager to take advantage of the light during the late afternoon sunshine.

George hung back behind us when we left the Fort to walk along Stacey Boulevard to the Gloucester Fisherman's Monument. He borrowed my Nikon to snap a few photos of us when Charles and I began to exchange stories about taking dance classes with Merce Cunningham. Olson had met the choreographer at Black Mountain College in 1955, and he gracefully demonstrated the way that Cunningham had taught him to walk with his weight distributed evenly on his two feet. After my daughter was born, I'd begun taking beginners' dance classes at the Merce Cunningham Studio. I'd looked up the address in the Manhattan Yellow Pages directory. I told Charles that on a recent morning in the studio I'd heard Cunningham explain the disaster of our current military involvement in Vietnam as the result of what he'd described as something having gone seriously wrong in the United States. Cunningham had told my dance class he felt that at some crucial time in America's short history, our nation's weight had been distributed incorrectly on its feet.

Strolling slowly back to the Fort, I used my Rolleiflex and Nikon cameras to photograph Olson when he stopped to chat with neighbors on the street and in their backyards. He paid no attention to me while I loaded roll after roll into the cameras, and he posed agreeably with the Atlantic Ocean as a backdrop when I asked him to. I was having such a good time that I hardly noticed the time going by, until the light was gone and Charles began talking about dinner.

George had given up on us by then. Charles suggested we eat at his favorite seafood restaurant in the Fort, where the waiters were his friends. I have a blurred memory of a large, nearly deserted restaurant, a table with a stiff, clean, white linen cloth, starched napkins, and lots of wine with the fish chowder. After dinner the two of us walked back through the Fort and climbed the steps to his apartment.

Once again Charles and I sat down on the straight-backed chairs around the kitchen table, this time to talk about painting. He filled our glasses with Cutty Sark from a new bottle he took out of the cupboard beneath the sink and settled down to tell me about the Gloucester painter Fitz Hugh Lane. Then we went on to talk about Turner seascapes and Mondrian abstracts. Our conversation drifted, as it usually did with Charles, to American history. I was intrigued by Olson's view of what he called our "total shift of consciousness" as a nation after the Civil War. We'd been drinking together for hours, and I began to find it difficult to concentrate. I'd been awake since dawn when I'd driven off to Gloucester, leaving Sam and Mallay still asleep in Brooklyn Heights. I began to find Charles's rapid jumps of associative ideas hard to follow.

By now it was midnight, too late to drive my car to find a hotel or a tourist home where I could spend the night, even if I hadn't drunk so much alcohol during the hours with Olson that I shouldn't drive at all. Feeling like a fool, I realized that in my eagerness to meet him, I had neglected to find a place to stay in Gloucester before I knocked at his door. I didn't know what to do. Olson suggested that I sleep in his study, and I accepted his offer immediately.

Unsteadily navigating the dark stairs outside at the back of the house, I returned to my car for my overnight bag. When I got back, I saw that Charles had found sheets and a pillow to make up a primitive bed on the cot in the room next to the kitchen. In his tiny bathroom I brushed my teeth, wiggled out of my sundress, and put on my nightgown in the cramped space between the washbowl and the toilet. I was exhausted from the hours of talk and the long drive.

Charles, just hitting his stride, said he'd come in and say goodnight. I put out the light and waited under the thin blanket on the cot, wondering what would happen next. I had drunk a lot of whiskey, and I really liked him. I needn't have worried. Olson stood beside my bed, bent over, kissed me softly on the cheek, and said, "I never came second to any man." I smiled with relief, he disappeared into his bedroom on the other side of the study, and I fell asleep instantly. I had discovered that the avant-garde giant I had been so apprehensive about meeting when I drove to Gloucester was also an old-fashioned gentleman.

In the morning I awoke before Olson, changed back into my sundress, and went next door to see if George or Ronni had made any coffee. George was working at an old desk with stacks of manila folders filled with typed and handwritten pages of Olson's manuscripts beside him. There were boxes of them piled everywhere in the apartment. I don't remember what we talked about until Olson woke up, any more than I can recall the two questions about Melville that I had come to Gloucester to ask Olson. I posed these last two questions to him when we went back to his kitchen, carefully wrote down his replies, and then told him I was ready to drive back to Brooklyn to finish my book.

Charles looked surprised, then turned to Butterick to say brusquely—and I never forgot his response in my embarrassment for George—"See, that's how to get things done. She doesn't come to me until she's done the work. This lady runs a tight ship, let me tell you." Nobody had ever said that about me before. My first, startled reaction was to ask Olson to explain exactly what he meant. Was it a compliment or a complaint? Quickly I decided to say nothing and take it as a compliment. I thanked Charles for his hospitality and left him talking to George at the kitchen table, just as I had found them twenty-four hours earlier.

When I visited Olson again at the end of July 1968, I had just sent off my manuscript of *Olson/Melville: A Study in Affinity* to Hawley, which he immediately gave to his printer. This time I drove back to Gloucester with Sam at the wheel of a huge, light-blue, chromium-decorated Plymouth station wagon. We had rented it to go sightseeing in New England with a family from London whom we'd invited to be our guests at the Newport Folk Festival before we drove up to Gloucester. An artist Sam was recording for Vanguard, the bluesman Buddy Guy, was performing in one of the concerts at Newport that year. After his show we went backstage into the performers' trailer and Buddy let our friends' wide-eyed twelve-year-old son hold his guitar.

Sam had taken along his portable Ampex tape recorder to Gloucester so that he could record Olson reading his long poem *Letter for Melville 1951*. First we found rooms in a tourist home on Stacey Boulevard across the street from the statue of the Gloucester Fisherman. After a supper of clam chowder in a downtown diner with shiny aluminum siding, which greatly impressed our English friends, we left them at the tourist home. Then Sam drove Mallay and me to Charles's apartment, first making a short detour to buy a bottle of Cutty Sark.

I stayed in the back bedroom with Mallay until she went to sleep in the middle of Charles's double bed, which had a very soft mattress and was only a few inches off the floor. Then I joined the company drinking whiskey around the kitchen table. This time Olson had another visitor, a Canadian journalist staying next door with Butterick. They helped us to set up the tape recorder and were an appreciative audience while Charles read his poem about Melville. Three years earlier, Sam and I had started a small press in New York City, which we called Portents. That summer we'd embarked upon a project titled "Melville in the Berkshires." We wanted to include a tape of Olson's reading in an edition of twenty-five paper boxes containing materials relating to Melville's life in his Pittsfield farmhouse, the place he wrote *Moby-Dick*.

While Olson was recording his poem, I heard an unexpected noise. It was the heavy thump of a solid weight hitting the floor. I'd never heard the sound before in my life. Charles—who had two children—recognized it. "That's your baby," he said. Greatly alarmed, I pushed back my chair and ran to the bedroom, expecting at any moment to hear Mallay start crying. To my great relief I found her still sound asleep on the rug after rolling off Charles's mattress.

It was nearly dawn when we returned to the tourist home. After breakfast, Sam brought me back to 28 Fort Square while he took Mallay and our guests sightseeing on Cape Ann. In the hours before Olson got up, I talked with Butterick. I showed him the photographs he'd taken of Charles and me walking together and talking about Merce Cunningham. I asked if I could use one of them on the dust wrapper of the Oyez study. George gave his permission, with the condition that I'd send him one of the portraits I'd taken of Olson.

Browsing through the heaps of folders in the open cardboard cartons while George was working at his desk, I noticed manuscripts relating to Charles's lectures at Black Mountain College. I separated out five pages about Melville, as well as many pages that seemed to be part of a series of lectures called "A Special View of History." I was reading them when Olson appeared, and I asked if I could borrow the pages where he discussed Melville for my book about the Olson/Melville affinity.

He agreed, and we went back to his kitchen where he made a pot of coffee. Then we went off for another of our walks so that I could take more photographs. I'd brought along some prints I'd made from our earlier session in June, and Charles said that he liked them, though he was surprised at how "grizzled" I had made him look. "You've really caught my physicality," he told me. This time while I took photographs he encouraged me to talk about my dreams.

Throughout the late summer and fall of 1968, Olson had a constant stream of visitors to his Gloucester apartment. Word got round that he was accessible to guests, and in his letters to me he mentioned the hippies who moved next door and invited him to their Frisbee parties. He also railed against the "whole police state" after the catastrophic debacle of the Chicago Democratic Convention to select the party's candidates for the 1968 presidential election.

There had been a major event in Olson's life in August 1968 soon after our visit: he met a gifted Swedish painter named Inga Lovén who had admired *Call Me Ishmael* and traveled to Gloucester to tape an interview with him about his writing and his Swedish ancestry. She visited him twice, stayed a total of three days, and made a big impression on him with her wit, intelligence, and charm. Charles fell in love with her, but Inga didn't reciprocate. At the end of the summer she returned to Stockholm when her mother became seriously ill. She and Charles exchanged many letters, and in 1970 her article on Olson was published in the Swedish literary magazine *Ord och Bild (Words and Images)*.

The following year, after Sam, Mallay, and I moved to Stockholm, Inga became our friend. We talked about Olson's poetry, and she played us the tapes of the interview she'd recorded with him. I helped her to transcribe the tapes, and we spent a lot of time together. I'd assumed that she and Charles had become lovers, but she insisted that they'd never had a physical relationship. Her tapes were marvelous. At one point we were especially moved to hear Charles say to her in a tone of wonder after they had talked for hours through most of the night, "Oh look, the sun's come up!"

On September 20, 1968, after I'd urged Charles to clarify what I couldn't grasp in our talks in Gloucester, he wrote me what he called an "Essay on the Matter Of," about the importance of the year 1875 in United States history. I'd sent him the Oyez black and white photographic announcement for the Olson/Melville book designed by the printer Graham Mackintosh, who designed many stunning small-press books in California. It featured my portrait of Olson standing in front of the expanse of the Atlantic Ocean near the Fort. Charles told me he'd shown the announcement to his daughter Kate when she visited him, and she was so fond of it that she took it away with her.

OLSON/MELVILLE: A Study in Affinity
by Ann Charters

This study, the first to be published on Charles Olson, discusses, significantly, the poet's first book, *Call me Ishmael*, his now famous creative response to Herman Melville. It also treats in depth Olson's other writings on Melville: his essays, reviews, and the poem "Letter for Melville 1951." Charles Olson has made available unpublished earlier essays on Melville from his Black Mountain College lectures in the 1950's; Mrs. Charters was able to discuss with Olson aspects of his involvement with Melville. The author's doctoral work at Columbia University was centered on Melville studies and she is now an assistant professor of English at New York City Community College. The book includes eighteen previously unpublished photographs of Charles Olson, his neighborhood and his Gloucester environment by Mrs. Charters. (Also by Ann Charters: *A Bibliography of Works by Jack Kerouac*. The Phoenix Bibliographies, 1967.)

Designed by Graham Mackintosh, the book will be available in two states: a clothbound edition to retail at $5.00; a paperbound edition, to retail at $2.50.

Available November 30th, 1968.

oyez Box 3014 Berkeley, California 94715

That autumn while my book about Olson was in press, I taught English classes at the college and worked on my statement about Melville in the Berkshires for the Portents project, which went slowly. My essay finally found its form in February 1969, after I heard John Cage read aloud one of his experimental prose constructs at a Cunningham dance program I attended in New York City. This was a month after Hawley airmailed me the first paperback copies of *Olson/Melville: A Study in Affinity*.

When I sent Charles the first copies of the Oyez book, he was focused on the publication of his new collection of Maximus poems, *Maximus IV, V, VI*, for which he had waited several years. I think he only glanced at my book before he telegraphed his congratulations. I'd warned him that I wasn't uncritical of his approach to Melville, and on March 7, 1969, after he'd taken the time to read my study, he blasted me. He was in a foul mood after being driven nearly mad by his isolation during an unusually severe Gloucester winter. Trapped in his small apartment during a succession of blizzards, he'd created this harrowing Maximus poem:

Full moon [staring out window, 5:30 AM March 4th
1969] staring in window one-eyed white round clear
giant eyed snow-mound staring down on snow-
covered full blizzarded earth after the
continuous 4 blizzards of February March   5 feet
of snow all over Cape Ann [starving
and my throat right from madness of isolation &
inactivity, rested hungry empty mind all
gone away into the snow into the loneliness,

bitterness, resolvedlessness, even this big moon
doesn't warm me up, heat me up, is snow
itself [after this snow not a jot of food left
in this silly benighted house   all night long sleep
all day, when activity, & food, And persons]
5:30 AM hungry for everything

Olson was right about the limitations of my analysis of *Call Me Ishmael*. I should have been more familiar with the full range of his writing before tackling the subject. I had been simple-minded enough to focus only on the specific ways he'd written about Melville, ignoring the fuller range of his ideas in his poetry and essays.

Olson didn't turn against me. My book was the only one that he could give to his Sicilian neighbors at the Fort. He thought enough of it to inscribe a copy to his landlord Paul Cardone on February 23, 1969. He approved of my book's introductory chapter, and he liked what Sam and I had accomplished with the Melville Box. In July 1969, Charles welcomed me back to Gloucester to celebrate the hardback publication of *Olson/Melville* with him.

Olson had sent me the folders of his Black Mountain College lectures on history, and in July I brought them back with my transcriptions, which I hoped to go over with him. Hawley told me he wanted to publish a second Olson book relating to Black Mountain after I'd included a postscript in *Olson/Melville* of excerpts from Charles's lectures relating to *Call Me Ishmael* given at the college in 1953 and 1956. When we met in Gloucester in July, Olson said that he wanted to think twice about a second book. He hadn't read his notes and lectures from Black Mountain for several years and was no longer certain of how they should be organized. His seclusion in Gloucester, as he wrote in his notebook on July 19, 1969, was also making him feel increasingly "Fussy, ill-tempered tired—exasperated."

It had been my impression that Olson had committed to the "Special View of History" project when he sent me his files containing this material from Black Mountain. He'd agreed that I could transcribe the manuscript pages relating to the series of lectures on history he'd given there. In preparation for the Black Mountain book I'd taped interviews with Robert Duncan in San Francisco about his experiences at the college. I'd also interviewed Robert Creeley, one of Olson's Black Mountain colleagues now living close by in Annisquam, Massachusetts, about his impressions of Olson as a teacher. I don't know what finally persuaded Olson to trust me, but later in July 1969, shortly after my visit, he telegraphed permission to go ahead with the project. Oyez published *The Special View of History: Charles Olson at Black Mountain College* in 1970. Unfortunately, by that time Olson wasn't alive to see it.

On September 29, 1969, I wrote my last letter to Charles, sending him a new Portents item, a prose sketch by Larry Eigner that Sam had illustrated. Confined to a wheelchair, Eigner was living with his parents in Swampscott, Massachusetts, not far from Gloucester. Sam and I had sometimes dropped by to see him after our visits to Olson, before our long drive back to Brooklyn Heights.

That autumn, to escape another long Gloucester winter in his apartment, Charles accepted a job teaching a graduate seminar in the English Department at the University of Connecticut in Storrs. The position had been arranged for him by George Butterick and the poet

Charles Boer, who were both employed there. Boer would go on to write a book about Olson in Connecticut, while Butterick arranged for the sale of Olson's papers to the University of Connecticut and dedicated himself to meticulously editing many of the manuscripts into prize-winning books.

Charles was happy to move to Storrs, telling Inga after he'd settled that he had "opened up such a situation here—and it is so beautiful." In rural Connecticut, he found himself far inland, many miles from the Atlantic Ocean. He felt drawn to the landscape because he appreciated the beautiful old stone walls lining the roads that connected the farmhouses and pasturelands surrounding the university. In a late Maximus poem, Olson wrote that the worn and weathered appearance of the stones made him feel a link with the area's primeval history.

Nearly five years later, when I accepted a teaching job at the University of Connecticut, I rented a house on Wormwood Hill Road in Storrs. Butterick told me that the particular stone walls that had impressed Olson enough to write a poem about them were located close to my house at the intersection of Mount Hope Road and Wormwood Hill Road, near where Charles had also lived for a time. Driving to and from campus I often passed these stone walls. The sight always brought to mind Olson's poem about them. Butterick included it as nearly the last poem in the edition of *The Maximus Poems* he prepared in 1983 for the University of California Press.

I live underneath
the light of day

I am a stone,
or the ground beneath

My life is buried,
with all sorts of passages
both on the sides and on the face turned down
to the earth
or built out as long gifted generous northeastern Connecticut
        stone walls are
as though they themselves were realms,

the stones they're made up of
are from the bottom such Ice-age megaliths

and the uplands the walls are the boundaries of
are defined with such non-niggardly definition

of the amount of distance between a road in & out
of the wood-lots or further passage-ways, further farms
are given

        that one suddenly is walking

in Tartarian-Erojan, Geaan-Ouranian
time and life love space
time & exact
analogy time & intellect time & mind time & time
spirit

the initiation

of another kind of nation

Several weeks into the semester in Storrs, Charles became unable to work. As he wrote Inga on November 11, 1969, "I've taken a job here. And it's holding me together. But my strength, which seems enormous sometimes, for moments or sometimes more, is still weak." After medical tests, he was diagnosed with liver cancer. By the time he was taken in an ambulance to New York Hospital in Manhattan, he was too ill for treatment. Sam and I heard that he was dying, but that he could receive visitors in the hospital. Early in January 1970, on a blustery winter afternoon, we rode the Lexington Avenue subway with Mallay to East 68th Street for our last conversation with Charles. Sam and I took turns staying with Mallay near the elevators in the hospital lobby so that each of us could say goodbye to him.

Since crowds of visitors were waiting in the corridor outside his room, we were given only a few minutes to spend with him. From his high white bed, supported by many pillows, Charles talked to Sam about the Maximus poems, which he said he'd finally finished in Storrs when he realized that he was dying. Charles described the last poem as being twenty-three pages long, but this manuscript was never found among his papers by Butterick and Boer, his literary executors.

When it was my turn to stand beside Charles's bed, I asked him to tell me about his dreams, because he had asked me to tell him about mine. He said that his dreams in the hospital weren't good anymore. "They've given me so much morphine in here that my wires are crossed."

He gallantly admired my new winter fur hat, which he thought was so handsome that it made me look like one of the Queen's guards. Before we said our last goodbye, he encouraged me to write down the great dream I'd had under morphine in another New York City hospital giving birth to Mallay. I had described this dream while I was photographing him in Gloucester during my visit in August 1968. "You know," Charles had told me, "you have a real talent for dreams."

Nearly two years earlier in our correspondence, Olson had offered to make a deal with me. If I didn't tell anybody about some missing books from Melville's library being located close to where I lived in Brooklyn Heights, he promised to explain how to find them if he didn't manage "to get to it soon" himself. This was a search he admitted he'd put off making since 1934, two years before I was born. Standing beside his bed in the hospital, I didn't have the heart to ask him about the specific location of the lost volumes.

During the short time we'd been friends, Charles had played an important role in my life. He'd been my "old courage-teacher" even before I realized that I'd been looking for one. His example had taught me, as I wrote to him on April 10, 1969, that criticism must be a creative act. The phrase "courage-teacher" comes from Allen Ginsberg's dream-encounter with Walt Whitman in "A Supermarket in California," another one of my favorite poems. Unlike Whitman, time had run out too soon for Olson. He died on January 10, 1970, two weeks after his 59th birthday. He had cherished his secret about how to find the missing books from Melville's library. I felt he should keep it for himself.

For my dear friends Dorothy and Robert Hawley

The Correspondence between Ann Charters and Charles Olson

Double brackets enclose material added by Ann Charters.

No spelling, punctuation, or capitalization has been altered except in cases where proper nouns were misspelled in the original letters.

90 State Street
Brooklyn, New York
January 7, 1968

Mr. Charles Olson
28 Fort Square
Gloucester, Mass.

Dear Charles Olson:

Robert Hawley of Oyez in Berkeley has asked me to write an essay about your work on Melville which he intends to publish this year, and for the past several months I've been reading and re-reading your Melville studies: *Call Me Ishmael; Letter for Melville 1951;* "David Young, David Old"; "The Materials and Weights of HM"; and "Equal, That Is, to the Real Itself." Judging from the titles listed in your bibliography, this seems to be the relevant material. Have I missed anything of yours on Melville in print?

What particularly impresses me is the fact that your serious involvement with Melville began so early—your interviews with the booksellers John Anderson, Jr. and Oscar Wegalin in 1934 (noted in Merton Sealts' *Melville's Reading*), and of course your personal scrutiny of Melville's notes in certain of his books—Shakespeare, the Owen Chase narrative, etc. If you have a moment and would care to describe some of the research you did at this time, or reflect on your earliest enthusiasm for Melville, I would be greatly interested.

Your bibliographers state that *Ishmael* is an extensive revision of your 1933 M.A. thesis at Wesleyan; Robert Creeley writes that you got a Ph.D. from Harvard. Did you continue your studies of Melville for your doctorate, or was *Ishmael* re-written after you'd left Wesleyan and Harvard, on your later Guggenheim grant? As you can see, I'm a little confused about chronology.

At what point did you realize the connection between Melville and your theories of projective space? In your essays about Melville since 1951, your orientation seems more toward examining his relation to your general philosophy, that is, [what you call] "Melville's redefinition of the real." Was it Lawrence and Dahlberg who led you to attempt, in *Ishmael,* to write as they had written about Melville, with "an animation the equal of Melville's animation"?

I hope these questions aren't impertinent or a bother—I wish it were possible to talk with you about Melville instead—but believe me very grateful for any help you care to give.

Sincerely,
Ann Charters

My dear Miss Charters,

I don't honestly know what hooked me on Melville. My father had given me *Moby-Dick* with some bad pun of his own rhyming cast your eyes and Mobylize when I was 17. My own sense of actually 1st reading it, with any sense—and that also is practically the last time!— was a winter here having just bought via John Grant the Bookseller Edinburgh George the IVth Bridge the Constable edition complete. For I think $25. In 1939. [Or 1938 probably. See later.]

It doesn't matter. The vivid entry was either Benito Cereno or Bartleby Middleton Conn spring 1933 getting out of the infirmary after weeks of illness, and [as it might be] starved, and throwing myself down finally on my own cot in my own room of a spring afternoon with the lovely Constable small edition of *The Piazza Tales*.

That did it. (It wasn't actually the Master's thesis nor any PhD)— I have none—it was a summer—what 1938?—doing a complete Melville & Shakespeare paper for F.O. Matthiessen. Dahlberg thought the section later published in *Twice a Year* was such, and I pulled it out the fall, 1938.

So it goes 1933-1938 really. I wrote a 1st version of a book by 1940. Which I showed to Dahlberg. Who then and there taught me how to write! (The mss. has since seen no one else's eyes.

Actually *Ishmael* is a great deal different than it even seems to be taken to be. But this of course I shall leave to yourself.

- - - - - - - - - - - - - - - - - - - -

I'm not aware I have or had in any sense drawn Melville toward any such "later" work of my own. My satisfaction, actually, with "Equal" etc. is rather that I do think that is the additional piece to *Ishmael* itself. [It may be of interest to you to know that Cape in London has just published *Ishmael* as one of the 1st four of the new Cape Editions, the other three being by Lévi-Strauss & Roland Barthes! [The Gallimard French translation appeared Paris earlier— 1963, I think.]

I also might emphasize what still Sealts even doesn't quite get or give the proportion of—Matthiessen does, much more, in his introduction to his own book *American Renaissance:* I had already, by the winter 1933-34, had the chance to examine all of Melville's library which had survived in the family. I was able to have the time to do this due to a grant arranged for me by Wilbert Snow, God bless him—a Fellowship, in Economics, no less, and in one of the finest slickest iced countryside I ever knew, Edward Matthews & I drove to East Orange New Jersey and came away, at the end of a Sunday afternoon, with 95 volumes of that library including the Shakespeare! [One of his granddaughters]

I may already have set out to retrace the sale, in New York, of Melville's library after his death. In any case the spring of '34—I was then 23—I succeeded. It was John Anderson (who had, in 1891, been a bookseller, but the founder, afterwards, of the Anderson Galleries, now Parke-Bernet—on now—?57th Street). He was the one who put me on to Oscar Wegalin, who had then—1891—been his delivery boy. What is exciting here is that there is a good chance more of Melville's books could be turned up if I could only go back to the work I had to leave then—1934 mind you!—taken no further!

OK. I hope this at least acknowledged your letter, and I do of course, the more that it is Hawley & yourself who are involved, hope the whole project succeeds utterly!

Yrs,
Charles Olson

28 Fort Square
Gloucester Wednesday January 10th [LXVIII
Write me again if I can be of any further use

90 State Street
Brooklyn Heights, N.Y.
Feb. 1, 1968

Dear Mr. Olson,

Please forgive the delay in acknowledging your letter—I just returned from a three week trip to San Francisco.

Thank you very much for your thoughtful reply to my letter about Melville. I shall ponder over what you have said, and with your permission I shall write you again in the near future if I have any more questions.

Sincerely,
Ann Charters

90 State Street
Brooklyn Heights, N.Y.
February 12, 1968

Dear Mr. Olson,

I have two small questions that still puzzle me about *Call Me Ishmael*—otherwise, while I neither claim to completely understand the book nor feel sure I'm taking it correctly, I'm about ready to begin the study for Oyez. With your kind patience, I now bring forth my questions.

What is the source for your introductory poem in *Ishmael* "O father, father/gone among. . ."

(also the other poem in In Cold Hell, Origin 8—"yr eyes, yr naiad/arms")? And

What is the meaning of the word dromenon (Fact #2)?

Your letter was a great help explaining your early involvement with Melville, and I notice that in *American Renaissance,* Matthiessen acknowledges your assistance in making Melville's library available to him (even if he later characteristically splits some hairs). That drive back from East Orange with 95 volumes of the Melville library must have been a triumphant occasion. After you showed the first version of *Ishmael* to Dahlberg in 1940, did the book sit in your mind and cook until your Guggenheim several years later, when you actually did the re-write? *Ishmael* is such a total performance that I find it hard to imagine it sitting still seven years. I would be very interested in the story of when and how you wrote the second version. Also, the typography in each of the section pages of the published book is so distinctive—FIRST FACT as prologue, <u>Call Me Ishmael</u>, etc.—you must have specified the book's layout and typography for Reynal and Hitchcock very precisely, much as with a poem. But these things you may not care to tell, and anyway, I've asked my two questions already.

Thank you again for writing me—

Best wishes,
Ann Charters

Dear Mrs. Charters,

Those are my own words, in the two instances you ask about. And as of <u>dromenon</u>, I quote you my original experience of the word—Miss Harrison's, and here, from her Home University Library small volume called *Ancient Art and Ritual,* page 35:

"The Greek word for a <u>rite</u> as already noted is <u>dromenon</u>, 'a thing done'—and the word is full of instruction. The Greeks had realized that to perform a rite you must <u>do</u> something, That is, you must not only feel something but express it in action, or, to put it psychologically, you must not only receive an impulse, you must react to it. The word for rite, <u>dromenon</u>, 'thing done,' arose, of course, not from any psychological analysis, but from the simple fact that rites among the primitive Greeks were <u>things done</u>, mimetic dances and the like. It is a fact of cardinal importance that their word for theatrical representation, <u>drama</u>, is own cousin to their word for rite, <u>dromenon</u>; <u>drama</u> also means 'thing done.' Greek linguistic instinct pointed plainly to the fact that art and ritual are near relations."

This is Harrison, 1913, in other words at the height of her work, *Themis* being published the year before.

Now, as of *Ishmael,* you are quite right it is one piece, and was written at a clip starting April 13th, 1945 and finished before the lst A-bomb, 1st week in August that same year. The only thing I didn't have 'right' was the opening Essex narrative, and I had left Washington and was in Newport the evening of the false Japanese armistice (Thursday of that week), and in Nantucket that weekend following. I wrote the opening story on the boat back from Nantucket the morning of Monday, must we say August 10th, that year. In other words, no connection to the ms. of 1940 at all. And in the interim—until April 13th, '45—I had been wholly absorbed in Foreign Nationality business & politics. (Actually, until November 1944 or right-date Jan 1st, 1945 when I set, in Key West, to write, like forever! [Wrote "The K," the go-away poem shortly after the Inauguration of that year.]

It gelled, as you also are aware, and I did 'set' it, for Harry Ford of Reynal & Hitchcock, with some rigidity. (It might interest you to know that something which the book is was immediately reflected in a cable from Sergei Eisenstein / on his receipt of the book through his former assistant, Jay Leyda / that John Huston held me in Hollywood in 1947 when he hoped to get Jack Warner to let him make *Moby-Dick*—and that Jean Renoir, there at that time, looked over the Essex part for a film by himself. —Crazy no? that the very men I wld have wanted to respond, in some curious "means" of the book itself, came down on me like shooting stars!

(I had hoped of course that the World would stand still!)

It has been a pleasure, and as well fun, to have you ask me these questions just at this time, and I come on so gabbily! Actually as you know the new two editions of the past year have equally put the book much in my hand again—and only yesterday read the *London Times* on the Cape Edition—calling the style a mishmash etc. (Exactly now, those years later, the response Eliot feared from the English when he turned it down from Faber even though Ezra had sent it to him as publishable simply as a "labor-saving device": no need to read *Moby-Dick* thereafter! Both he and W.C. Williams being death on Herman anyway!

(Also, if I didn't tell you before, that Gallimard bought the book in 1947, at the same time they bought one from Henry Wallace, and for the same price—$250! I treasured that check!)

I still stress that books of Herman Melville's library, with writing in his own hands, are in fact right around the corner practically from yourself. So keep an eye peeled, if your interest is any more than tossing off this article for Bob Hawley!

Good luck, and if something further shld rise or occur to you don't mind asking me. I am spending a winter catching up with 'paper' so it is no chore, and in fact a pleasure to have you come in from that quarter. And I shll eagerly look forward to what you do write.

Yrs, confidently,
Charles Olson

(28 Fort Square, Gloucester
Massachusetts, February 14th
/'LXVIII

PS: I wish I hadn't run out of the Cape Edition of *Ishmael* simply that it is the 1st time it has been reset in English since the original (both the Evergreen and the City Lights editions are photo-offset, and to see it re-set—there was a sort of square or futura condition in Harry Ford's choice of font and weight of type which wasn't altogether to my longing. —I read the Cape Edition for the 1st time practically as tho I too was a Reader!

PS2: The way the book continues to live is like wildlife—& that is also the advantage possibly of such a subject. And such a wild: I take an eagle's guilt etc

90 State Street
Brooklyn Heights, N.Y.
February 18, 1968

Dear Charles Olson:

Thank you for answering my questions and confirming some
of my hunches about *Ishmael.* I am very intrigued by your hint that
books from Melville's library—with notes in his own hand—are
"in fact around the corner practically" from where I live. Melville's
granddaughter let you drive off with 95 of the 219 volumes Sealts said
have been located—and now you say you know of more! Wouldn't
anyone who still possesses Melville's books have told Harvard or the
Berkshire Athenaeum or some such Institution about them?

Please tell me more. My interest in Melville—and Olson—began a
long while before Bob Hawley and I contracted a study of *Ishmael,* and
I'm sure it will continue a long time after my article is written. I can of
course <u>walk</u> right around the corner practically any time, but there are
lots of corners in sight.

With best wishes,
Ann Charters

OK?   [[postmarked Gloucester, Feb. 27, 1968]]

Yes, & let me hear how you come along on the writing thing, O.

[Shrove Tuesday, 1968]

I didn't mean to hold you up on that search for more of Melville's
<u>own</u> books,

but if I've put it off myself for 34 years you'll believe me I'd like
still to do it?

I'll make a deal with you: keep what I sd to yrself [that is, its
proximity to yourself], and if I fail to get to it soon I'll let you know?

[[90 State Street, Brooklyn Heights, N.Y.]]
March 2, 1968

Dear Charles Olson,

Of course you ought to continue the trail of Melville's books by yourself—34 years is only a wink of the eye in the millennium. I wondered when you mentioned the books again in your second letter, but I rose to the bait because I love Melville too—& to find more of him near where I live in Brooklyn Heights! Your deal is on, & whatever happens let me know.

This past week has taken me deep into the Oyez book on *Ishmael*. I'm very excited by what I'm finding as I write, especially the references to Melville in your other published work. In the Berkeley lecture you mention the cannibalism in *Ishmael*'s preface, and there's also the sentences on Cooper, Melville & the American experience in "A House Built by Cpt. John Somes." I'd never related your interest in Colonial documents, esp. John Smith's literary style, and your style in the three *Ishmael* "Facts." There's of course so much more—I'm sure I'm finding only a small part of it. But these discoveries are making the slow passage of winter into spring outside my window go much quicker.

I hope Gloucester is also near spring. You have my best wishes and my continuing interest in whatever you want to tell me about Melville.

Sincerely,
Ann Charters

28 Fort Square Gloucester
March 6th [[1968]]

My dear Ann Charters,

It is a pleasure to have you finding those strings, of the "web" (and I hadn't of course thought or knew in that sense of any of them— though know both that Berkeley spin-off, and the funny piece, for Gino Clays on the Somes house, are 'loaded.' Though in two different ways—like maybe a composer feels—one a shriek-out and the other home performance 8 mm! for sure! with that difference.

It is also a strange and lovely experience you sense yourself, to have you writing a book on *Ishmael* at the same time this year I'm trying to dub something out myself [I don't mean of course on Melville. Or Ishmael!] That Hawley! I suddenly also realize he is accomplishing something he has forever been seeking, the way he holds to CMI [[*Call Me Ishmael*]]—and has said so, so long.

So what is so nice is your way of doing it, and if, as it goes, any other questions come up which you think I might give a flip or turn to, do of course ask me.

I write in the midst of a good day here, one of several. Yet I yearn for the winter to be over the dam and March, which I used to find particularly beautiful here, be come.

> Just to let you know the
> pleasure of hearing how it does
> go,
> O. Charles Olson

90 State Street
Brooklyn Heights, N.Y.
March 12, 1968

Dear Charles Olson:

Another question does come to mind about *Ishmael*—when you conceived its organization, did you have in mind any idea of argument in terms of geometry, some concept of non-Euclidean proof?

i.e. Fact I, Parts 1 and 2, Fact II, Parts 3 & 4, Last Fact. Part V Conclusion. Q.E.D.

What little geometry I remember is Junior High Euclid— propositions, axioms, theorems, etc. Most of it faded out of memory now. You write so knowingly about 19th century mathematics in "Equal, That Is" that I wonder if perhaps you were doing something freely geometrical in *Ishmael*. On the other hand, perhaps my radar is completely off beam here. *Ishmael* is of course a projective space essay. Is there even such a thing as non-Euclidean proof? I won't bring it up if you don't.

If you care to help, I'm most grateful. Your last letter was very kind. Thinking about *Ishmael* is a great pleasure, and Hawley is very much on your side.

                    With best wishes for
                    your Spring work,
                    Ann Charters

28 Fort Square Gloucester
Massachusetts
[[March 15, 1968]]

My dear Ann,

No, that one, got away from me—if there was any such
chance (of such composition). —The idea though of non-Euclidean
composition—like polytopes—wow! (*Projective Geometry* I suddenly
realize was the title of Coxeter's book. Which I did read, in the Library
of Congress—but that was for sure after I had met Cagli again—after
the War—& was doing Tarots, & he had told me about this Fellow,
Armenian, Haltford, who had no education because he worked so long
for his father selling rugs; and who had this vision, or of course dreams,
of all the polytopes man can now possibly imagine—and no one had
ever, until he dreamed them, ever thought of them before!

So you see there are those mad possibilities quite within the
rational (or what I now call the dogmatic) nature of experience: in so
many words, "truth" like the word is—or was.

It is a particular pleasure, to hear from you again—and delightful
of course that *Ishmael* is working for you still. I can certainly verify to
you that it was in fact its composition—that is, I mean the number,
& order of its parts which were the thing which (I suppose) was so
much all I did want somehow it to be that that together explains most
probably the 'waiting' to write it until etc. That is, I certainly can recall
the care with which I went to the Smithsonian and got Remington B.
Kellogg strictly & directly to instruct me in whale habits & food—and

that my mind was <u>already</u> set to have that "color" or knowledge there that way (as it is) exactly—like so much pinch of ginger etc. and that kind of mixing. —And you know what I wrote you about the opening narrative. So it <u>was</u> certainly these "parts" or substances-in-space which were my interest: The writing itself seems never to have been, my memory at least is, much of the business—at least so far as sort of waiting for <u>that</u> in the oven!

Anyway, crazy to have you have me <u>thinking</u> about these things now (when for the <u>life</u> of me I no more any longer figure I can in fact practically write in prose at all (!)—and parallelly sp? can only almost impossibly for simply anything that I can get <u>said</u>, in such a way the words fall sort of or somewhat satisfyingly to some other scale of order entirely—"truth" itself for example almost exclusively!—if there <u>is</u> such.

OK. Not to keep going on but equally to make evident to you in acknowledgment to your questions again how much you do turn to the face of that clock as in fact I read time from it too!

Love & all best further
wishes & concerns
O (Friday am March 15 ['LX8]

[[90 State Street, Brooklyn Heights, N.Y.]]
April 10, 1968

Dear Charles,

On April 16-18, my husband and I will be in Gloucester, mostly to take some pictures of Dogtown, but also on the chance that I might meet and talk with you. I don't know if you'll even be in Gloucester at this time—I heard you were planning a trip to California early in April—but this is the only time I have to get away, so I'll take a chance on finding you home when I call.

I hope we're fortunate enough to see you, and that you'll have a minute or two to talk.

Best regards,
Ann Charters

[[90 State Street, Brooklyn Heights, N.Y.]]
April 30, 1968

Dear Charles,

Very sorry to have missed you in Gloucester two weeks ago—I hear you are only now making your way back from California. I don't blame you for not rushing back—the past winter lasted at least two months too long. Instead of talking with you as we hoped, we spent the day walking on Dogtown Common—with our Irish setter—to our (not the dog's, who was not amazed) simultaneous great pleasure & amazement. It is a wonderfully deserted landscape—except for the rocks with the strange carved inscriptions, so straight: "Never try, never win." "Be on Time." The affect was madness. Who did them? Some seem old, others looked as if carved only last month. And all of them free from vandal's painted initials, etc. despite the empty shotgun cartridges everywhere on the ground. Many ghosts. Stranger still. How extensively settled was Dogtown in the past—was it mostly grazing land or actual homesteads? Very sad to see some signs of new interest/ destruction in the landscape—we noticed recent road work & an ominous fire hydrant, alas. I hope nothing comes of this, at least not before the next tidal wave.

These days I'm revising and retyping my study of your writing on Melville—Hawley would like the completed ms. by the end of May, but this may be a little too soon. Two more questions in my mind: do you care to tell me who the "Letter for Melville" was originally written to? And did some of your ideas in parts 3 & 4 of *Ishmael* arise from reading Freud's *Moses and Monotheism*? If you read this before *Ishmael,* was it around 1939-40, or before writing the final version in 1945? I hope you don't find these questions irrelevant, and if you have the time or inclination to answer, I am very grateful.

I'd still like to talk with you about Melville, & other matters,* before I send my book off to Oyez. Perhaps some weekend in the next few weeks would be possible, or—if you don't have plans to be away—a weekend early in June. Spring is passing much too quickly, nearly out of sight, but there would be time to return to Gloucester if you were planning to be away this summer.

Best wishes,
Ann Charters

*Other Matters: like, why the date 1875? —"Around that date man reapplied known techniques of the universe to man himself. . . ." I think I understand theoretically what you're getting at—but I'm not sure I understand what <u>particular</u> men & books you have in mind. All this is after *Moby-Dick,* I know; my concern right at the moment is with Melville, but Olson is also there. I wouldn't bring this up now, except I've been thinking about it & I'm unable to find any published things of yours on the subject.

P.S. Third Melville question: You were into Melville & *Moby-Dick* as a Wesleyan student—finding his notes on Shakespeare was perhaps the first big discovery. Did you realize what there was in "The Tail" chapter at this time too, or was this a later discovery?

June 16? 1968
Brooklyn Heights

Dear Charles,

The Hotel Savoy has an imposing façade, but no contest: the most generous hospitality in Gloucester is at Charles Olson's.

Many, many thanks for a beautiful two days—

Ann Charters

[[white gift card]]
June 20, 1968

Dear Charles,

These [[cartons of cigarettes]] come to you elegantly gift-wrapped from the Times Square cigar store where Ed Sanders once worked & watched the Toe Queens.

Again, many thanks for the lovely talks—

Ann Charters

[[Tinted postcard of Italian fishing boats, Gloucester, Mass.

Postmarked Gloucester June 28, 1968]]

[[In red ballpoint pen ink]]

My dear Ann—Just so you'll have word as well as what I promised—& for the several things you've sent—and brought: think still much of Turner Mondrian etc. Please let me hear, O

Fri. June 28 FIESTA

[[In green ballpoint pen ink]]

+ Virchow's rooms

Berlin, —correction,

Adolf Bastians, & 1895

—and so the date you asked about The

Popular Science Monthly, Issue

January, 1878

Dear Charles,

I've thought of you often & wanted to write—I've been finishing the book & printing the photographs to go into it. Hawley thinks it/ they are great. He's flying me to SF this Thursday to prod Graham Mackintosh into setting it right now. EUREKA!

Your card was exquisite. The true spirit of the June fiesta. Later this summer I hope to show you Sam and baby Charters.

Keep Kool—it's horribly hot here. What is the name of the slip of beach near the Fort where we walked?

Best,
Ann Charters

90 State Street
Brooklyn, New York
August 7, 1968

Dear Charles,

Pardon for the delay in thanking you for the great night at 28 Fort Square. I'm sorry Sam missed learning how to eat steamed clams, but we joined in the enjoyment of the conversation and the brandy. I wish Brooklyn Heights wasn't so many hours from Gloucester. I miss the sea breezes—we didn't swim until the next day, when we were back at Newport (no time before)—and the talk.

The papers enclosed are your Black Mountain College lecture notes, which I Xeroxed, and some other items you might like to look at. We publish Portents—records and printed things. The letter on the Semina cover is meant to be read, almost like a Maximus letter. (?)

Hawley wrote today to send samples of the type Graham is using on the Olson/Melville book, and I'm supposed to be getting page proofs—already!—any day now. The book almost wrote itself out of my mind, that smoothly, very little revised, so that it's strange to face it again in print. It's as if somehow it got written down in spite of itself.

I've just looked at the new U of Chicago [[Press]] edition of *Billy Budd,* which cavalierly denies the validity of Freeman's edition of "Baby Budd Sailor." Regardless of whether this is true or not, this angers me, for I romantically incline toward your evaluation in the "David Young" piece. But we see yet again the instance of using a dead man's hand to scratch the academic's back. Let us find more of

Melville's books, and leave his texts alone!

If the book on Black Mountain College doesn't include your lectures, I'd be interested in editing them with you. I was disappointed to hear you'd sent them off to Butterick, especially after he had told me at your house that he didn't think they were worth republishing, since your thought had matured so much since you'd written them (!) and since you'd published all the ideas in subsequent essays anyhow (!!) That I'd estimated the lectures very differently you know from my having asked your permission to quote from two of them in my study; when I talked with Hawley three weeks ago in California, he was interested in publishing a book of them. Also, if you could get hold of the tape masters of the recording you did a few years back in the Boston studio—and liked the sound of so much—Portents would be very pleased to buy it and bring it out right off. And, if you've a minute for the letter on the significance of the date 1875 you <u>owe</u> me, I'd like to hear about it. Why not 1791?

Enough. Be well, Charles, and thanks again for a beautiful evening.

Ann Charters

PS: I forgot to tell you that Hawley said you spent a night reading the Tarot for him, and that it was fantastic. In Kentfield, California last time I met Antoninus, who is deep into horoscopes, which are too microscopic for me. I relented and read his palm that afternoon, and it was very sunny.

Ann

Forgive me. But as you might imagine the excitement of having
a chance to work again even though actually I have had the steadiest
stream of visitors I have ever known—or next-door neighbors (like the
new Gloucester hippies at 38 etc. with whom I played Frisbie yesterday

in any case plus plus I simply <u>must</u> thank you thus without one
more days delay for <u>all</u> yr delicious presents—including Sam's & your
own book together—and your photographs

(I <u>wish</u> I might be free to send you the photo of Dogtown I was
given last night by Otis Riggs: taken when his Aunt Grover was a
maiden lady—D'tn herself as we all like to re-mem-ber-her!

Just then to get back, & please write (and send <u>more</u> said he the
pig—& love to your beautiful baby, & Sam

Charles Wed. Aug. 28th

(over)

PS: I <u>think</u> I've had 15 minutes to myself here this summer! /hid
tonight, though it is 10:10,—have the shade down & am plotting to
wash up or something personal-like. (I have also fallen in love but alas

the lady went back to the continent & I don't even know whether—I
don't even think she loves me as much as I do her.

 Which is impossible condition (this is for yr own <u>private</u> ear,

 O

[[Back of envelope]] And <u>of course</u> Bill Everson has a sunny palm
the Bakersfield Idiot who needs his flagellance like a hole in the head
(through which his rhetoric pours out when it cld have been if he
weren't so convinced he can't afford to be sunny; it'd been poetry. Have
found the name of the Denver studio film—Also did Chekhov 1875
matter—And <u>not</u> 1791, 1763! So keep me at it till you get everything.

[[28 Fort Square, Gloucester, Mass.]]
[Saturday night September 14th: [[1968]]

Annie

I have just now read the '5th week' [or 5 pp. thing you had, & sent back]—& realize of course what interest it must have been for you to find me at that date 'teaching' secrets of like Ishmael—I mean both as of the year [Thursday May 3rd 1956 (?)] and as of your having filled your own book before running into this [1968]

Did you therefore have in mind to 'add' it to the book in press? [Question #1]

But the other reason I write is the real one: that I <u>had</u> not (I believe) responded to your opinion, & desire to use what had got called the Pleistocene material (vis-à-vis Butterick & Hogg's opinion of it etc)

The point rather is, that the piece you had here [the 5 pp. 5th week] was from a wholly different 'series' or 'group'—

& that which got called *A Special View of History* I think it was then called.

And so—if your interest or some purpose holds—let me know —and you cld examine the full 'charge' of notes (in case you were so minded).

Excuse handwriting (scratching this out in the midst still of lousy housekeeping & poor distracted living [visitors or these new newly made children or people of today who have no distinctions other than what they make themselves. Which is fair enough. (I'm not myself still doing any different (like, at 57

But the denigration (if that's the word—the struggle against the society which this seems to involve them in, is all waste for me. I mean I got work to do, & can't hold hands even if it's a rosie round the whole police state

                    Love & best to your own
                    O

Keep me posted on how the <u>Affinity</u> book goes! Yrs like 'for it'

                    Charles

[[90 State Street, Brooklyn Heights, N.Y.]]
September 19, 1968

Dear Charles,

Now it's <u>1763</u>! 1875, 1791, 1763—why not 1630, the Puritans & Galileo? You haven't arrived at the dates from pulling them, like silk scarves, out of your side pockets, certainly. What's on your mind? Please tell me more . . . everything!

About the Denver studio fellow—if you supply his name & address, we'll approach him with the idea of releasing your record on Portents—or you could tell him you have a definite production offer from us. Whatever you think best. We're very interested & feel it should come out, especially since you liked that performance & that studio sound. We are up to Portents #10—this Larry Eigner piece, published last week, with plans for [[John]] Wieners next, and then— my special project—a Melville box, a sort of construct/collection of things from his Berkshire years. A very limited edition—now if we could only include in every box a book from his Arrowhead library.

I was very excited finding the BMC mentions of the genesis of *Ishmael* in your lecture notes last June. I guess I didn't make clear their significance to the "Affinity" study when I asked you about them—but the 5 pp. have been added to the book now at the printers, as a Postscript separate from my discussion. I introduce them with 2 paragraphs—I said the 5 pages were "the first of 3 drafts of a statement that would eventually be published as the essay 'Equal, That Is.' In its first version, the essay was read to a class preceded and followed by the study of A.N. Whitehead's *Process and Reality*." And then your 5 pp. finish the Postscript—and my book. I hope this way of handling the material was OK. You can see from the Oyez flyer that your things are described very generally.

But my interest in the <u>full</u> charge of the notes most certainly holds. At your place that memorable morning, I looked through your folders at the same time chattering at Butterick, & there was much in that series I didn't have time to read. It must have been a sharp focused eye that saw what it did in them about Melville, since I had so little time & there was such a mountain of folders. I would love to examine the lecture series more carefully—please—if you could possibly send them, or Xeroxed copies, it would be great. There is, I think, much there to get into. And perhaps put this material together for publication. IT SHOULD BE PUBLISHED. It's great, rich stuff, containing many insights into your work.

Perhaps with the end of summer will come also the end of the visitors—& in the weeks before the real cold, you will enjoy working uninterruptedly—except for the odd Frisbee, & the stray scratch on your kitchen window after you've pulled the shades. Why not interest the Gloucester councilmen in the worthwhile project of transporting one of the carved boulders from Dogtown to your doorstep, one with some legend to discourage the kids—like "If Work Stops, Values Decay." Or, simply, "Study." You could add your own exclamation point.

Sam has looked over, hands me brandy, & mutters, "Writing, writing, writing." It's too much fun—I wish we could <u>visit</u>—but I alas am back [[teaching]] at the college & should find words to describe the Puritans for American Lit I. Just learned that Dahlberg is teaching this same course at nights at "my school"—but he couldn't be, it couldn't be the same course. I will tune in tomorrow, & find out.

Love,
Annie

<u>Friday September 20th</u> [[1968]]

Dear Ann—

Thanks for that crazy package today—1st photo of Larry [[Eigner]], & the delightful inclusion of the works of that unknown Beast standing (where? How come you were able to get <u>that</u> shot?)

I will enclose the Denver man's letter—& see what you & Sam can do [I only hope you don't awake his greed, or old frustration—I mean on his <u>series</u>, not just myself alone; & some back-grief or piss-off over Stan Brakhage (who was responsible, ultimately, for the idea).

I also welcome your idea of looking over the whole back-load of material—like you say, "from the 50s." —It will certainly put you in whatever they mean by the cat-bird's seat. That is, I'm sure the material wld be most successful if severely (practically) edited.

In any case to get it started why don't I just take the chance (with the mails, I mean) and ship you the 'rest' of the Serial or Special View of—and give you the chance to see if that does satisfy interest you.

And then [as soon as Glover has out the 'letters' I seem to have written—to Jack Clarke [who took over my seminar which that year was to be Pleistocene when I cut out in the fall of 1965] we can then judge whether or not Butterick and or Hogg [who both took that seminar] have any right to their differing impression than your own— or mine: that is, I'd <u>not</u> have proposed such a theme still in <u>1965</u> if I did not still 1968 think a book of essays called <u>Pleistocene</u> isn't like or put it around the other way Lower [or is it Upper?] Paleolithic?

Love,
Charles

And I'll end all questions on dates if once more you'll write to me & say what you do mean. And give me the latest word on the <u>Affinity</u> book—Sounds too much,

O

[[on the back of the envelope]]

<u>Saturday</u>

PS Can't at the moment lay my hands on the Denver fellow's letter. Will therefore shoot this because it's for you anyhow—+ follow with that other enclosure when I can —O

Essay on the Matter of,
for Ann Charters Friday
September 20th (1968)
8:20 to 9:35 PM

Actually by "1763"—or 1765 I am striking at what I take to be daily now showing up more and more: that the 18th Century virtues, both of the Social Contract and the Liberal Education (cf. Founding catalog of King's now Columbia College sometime around date (later than, 1763?—in other words, the Declaration of Independence and the Articles of Confederation (as used of course and in particular the Constitution—like, any day now: example, the incredible (to me) suspicion, on the part of all the liveliest young for some time now, that the Courts too are sold out—

I come back: that there was something went on around some date like 1763 (or 1765) which did rigidify into the Revolution itself and an enormous 150 years plus of a life not yet sufficiently or accurately re-known started to become something Cooper (for example, in *Homeward Bound*—date?—or my own particular favorite (of that older America of the Proclamation Line plus) *The Prairie*, 1826, an extraordinary book still—actually, as you may well know, laid, in its action, on the North Platte in the Sioux Country of the terrifying post-Civil War events which finished the Indian in America—1877 date Crazy Horse's bayonetting by a jumpy U.S. cavalry guard: that is I am suggesting "the Colonies" (not in the sense we have of them as pre-the Independence but them as the life in America from the 17th

(with considerable impetus from the 16th & 15th century) but take it
from the English settlement on (again, though, now it is going to turn
out to be imperative that French, and to that degree Spanish which
Mexican is—as well obviously especially now as Negro slave trade to
the Caribbean area as early as the Hawkins family's almost personal
invention of it: add now American Indian procession (plus—la-la-
Pleistocene—30,000 BC is it everybody now is getting aghast at:
Elephant Hunters Clovis site near Dallas proved out, 1956, at more
than 37,000 BP) acid-rock like your husband too wld say I imagine
as—or like all these costumes and kooked-out Aborigines giving
spiritual cover—Cooper's Moneyking, Chain-bearers! Country Joe
and the Animals. Big Pencil.

not for God's sake to plug all this in. You'd imagine I think it is
not so 'easy.' All I am though trying to stress is the discouragement
Cooper felt—& registered, so early, and with such interest—had
already overtaken this Country within 50 years of the Revolution—
And what he turned to—the 'crime' of Ishmael Bush

hear that Early Melville (!!-!- his Prairie, as the preface to the John
Marr Constable Collected vol. Poems pp. 199 & 200 in particular—
plus 201 & 202

pure U.S. Grant, "Leadsville" I want to say, Ohio (as in fact
Melville's prairie, Galena, Illinois—and Grant's brothers' store, 1861,
where was it?

: I think in fact progress is the totally wicked sense of not having
lived at all (it is Columbia's 1st catalogue which so outrageously states

the virtues of a liberal education which have now so involved all
ownership in America—plus those who <u>own</u> the things ownership so
greedily supplies—<u>in the total hypocrisies of same</u> (virtues it seem wld
still break my heart (see sleeve I wrote to record <u>Wilbur Snow</u> (reads
his poetry) Bert & I or some Boston-to-Maine record company) 1961)
to see the America which was once <u>continuous</u>, and <u>continuing</u>, <u>finally</u>
stuffed in the (certainly this is my <u>emphasis</u> on the year 1763) ground
by and after the Civil War: Why I make so much for a search for a date
<u>out</u>

(fr. Notebook dated July 18th 1966)	CONTROL DATE IS = January, 1878 issue of POPULAR SCIENCE MONTHLY <u>that date</u>	assassination of Crazy Horse is September 5, 1877— Sioux moved from Nebraska agencies to Missouri River fall 1877

In other words what I am seeking to offer you is a "group" (in
what I believe is a good mathematical sense) which go   <u>to 1763</u>
and continuing on through like <u>December 1877</u> at which point a
development ("migratory" <u>centrifuge</u> of a previous "<u>rose</u>") ran out of
the ground on the blanket Crazy Horse was placed down on that night
his blood soaked through—age, like ————————28!

And then <u>jump</u>, out of it, since: or things die. There was a great
reach-around with and about January 1878

So if I then—simply to end my own mind's content, and give you
my earliest & <u>best</u> key—

Of the unraveled rose—the human race previous to the modern migratory movement was at rest (duration-point, in the "motion" sense which is of course constant (and thus can mean existence—in other words, nothing) up through a date that side of the Carpini mission to Karakorum, 1247-1249?)—in any case high last points (like Crazy Horse's death—or HM's *Confidence Man* written before his departure on Holyland trip 1856? (or *Pierre* or Cooper *Homeward Bound,* 1838) last points of earlier rose to that which we still call America were say St. Francis like 1224 (?) & Al 'Arabs' Meccan Revelations—same approximate date (Friar Carpini was St. Francis' 1st political convert & agent (to Germans, I believe 1st (while possibly St. Francis was still alive;—and that whirl of the time-shape had lasted from sometime not too long after Mohammed's death, and the earliest activity of the Norse: I use 793, & 808 first Norse attacks on traders; and Al Jahir (Gehu) approx. 800 to make that one—and the prior one to the one we have known best (so far as I can see into the mist man makes around time when it is not that misty)

[[September 23, 1968]]
Epigraph for the "Argument" within the "Matter" written for you:

John Adams himself—Notes written by himself beside passages in Court de Gébelin's *Mode Primitif*—therefore possibly the earliest real beginnings of what I realize today may in fact (that is, the dates after 1763 until a new way had to be found—after Crazy Horse was punctured: the protest (of the Protestant America and Revolution):

"The beginning of the 19th Century has been de Movais Augure"

"The Age is not come. The Order is not arranged.

The reign of Saturn has not yet been born.

You must have lived many years after 1800 to celebrate

such Facts in your divine Numbers."   [underlining mine]

(! My exclamation: sometime after   it has been, year 1968

"Something mysterious, however, under all this"

"I call it spirit and I know what I mean as well as he does"

"Americans! Have a care. Form no schemes of universal empire.

The Lord will always come down and defeat all such projects."

"Let the human mind loose. It must be loose. It will be loose."

(Copies from use made of them by Robert Duncan in "Passages 32")

[90 State Street
Brooklyn Heights, N.Y.]
9/23/68

Dear Charles,

NOTES FROM ABOVE THE GROUND:

Working today in the NYPL Rare Bk room, I found a poem
that Maximus must not miss. Written about ten years ago by Ernest
Cummings Marriner, in appreciation of that "Gloucester master-writer of
the sea," J.B. Connolly. To wit:

Do you know of Tommy Clancy & the stalwart Wesley Marrs?

Have you heard the sails aflappin & the creakin of the spars?

Have you followed Cpt. Wesley in the able LUCY FOSTER,

As he smashed the fastest records out of Reykjavik to Gloucester?

Do you know the crazy exploits of the WICKET CELESTINE

That turned completely over in the storm-infested brine?

Have you heard of Patsie Oddie with his unrelenting pride?

"To hell with them that's saved," said he, "here's to them that died."

Do you know how Maurice Blake, sir, with the help of Tommy Clancy,

Sailed a race made memorable with every thrill that's chancy?

When the ship rode out a hurricane with every spar a-sweal,

Rode home indeed upon her rail & her crew out on the keel?

You know them not, but wish you could before another year?

Then read the books of Connolly while yet you have them near.

And then you'll know the Crow's Nest talk & how the FOSTER ran,

And feel the zest of all that's best in Connolly's Gloucestermen.

(File perhaps under 42ND STREET INTELLIGENCE. Did you know they chose the *Auerhahn Maximus* as 1 of the 50 prettiest bks of the decade?)

Love,
Annie

Charles—

Do you know of *The Teachings of Don Juan: A Yaqui Way of Knowledge* by Carlos Castaneda (U. of Calif. Press, 1968)? If you don't, shall I send you a copy?—it's out of sight!

Annie

I <u>do</u> have the Yaqui book—it is now
3:00 AM of the lst of October [[1968]]

Annie,

Well, if you won't write me back (soon enough for me) I'll
write you <u>further</u> on <u>that subject-matter</u>, the Federal-democratic
interregnum, 1776-1826, and <u>then</u> what <u>began</u> even though it does not
'occur' in that important sense of 'entering history' [which is when an
impetus already long existent becomes, I suppose, a momentum].

My own interest, as you'd guess, is of course in those prior
occurrences—or what I call 'primacies' when the thing—any 'thing'—
really 'begins.'

And what I wrote you 12 days ago did 'short' that <u>better-part</u> of
the story [as of its emergence, coupled to the Sioux's utter defeat—the
final essential "deficit" of the Continental environment, in Charles
Peirce's "How To Make Our Ideas Clear," in *Popular Science Monthly*,
New York, <u>January 1878</u>, p. 293.] The soul and meaning of thought
(he says, there) can never be made <u>to direct itself towards anything</u> [my
underlinings, throughout] but <u>the production of belief</u> (first man, since
Plato kicked it—to restore <u>dotha</u> [dogma=<u>judgment</u>, as in <u>the series</u>,
action]. Parallel thought in movement has thus for its only possible
motive the attainment of thought at rest. But when our thought about
an object has found its rest in belief, <u>then our action on the subject can
firmly & safely</u> begin. Beliefs, in short, <u>are really rules for action;</u> and
the whole function of thinking is but <u>one step in the production of
habits of action.</u> (! End of metaphysics—& beginning of . . . .

I just, actually, come to think of it, only need to put you yourself in mind of what you, actually yourself, have long seen, was where I did bring the 'preparation for' this arrival point out into the, open: that is, the "Real Itself" piece, in the *Chicago Review*'s Zen issue, Summer 1958—the opening 'argument,' there, that 'a change' had taken place, & could be dated with a number of successive primary actions, taken in the mind of a file of men starting with Keats just about the date of H. Melville's birth.

That, in fact, was about what I meant to write you tonight—the fill-in on the 50 years, just about, immediately running forward after the American Revolution as such had had its shot; and that something more—something of a more interesting form of belief—had to obtain; and, in the past week or so, I have had occasion to see more if that 'thesis'—that somewhere around Cooper's *Prairie* an end and a beginning were sheer. It seems so: if I take, say, Noah Webster's 1st edition of his *Dictionary* [I think of him, and of his *Dictionary,* as one of the signal 'American things'—

I sent off a long 'ugly' poem, since just about when I last wrote you, to the new *Stony Brook* a Journal of Poetry, and when you see it you will notice the same emphasis there, on Webster (even though it is there used to tie Hawthorne and the Gloucester painter Fitz Hugh Lane, both born a generation's half-life earlier than Mr. Melville, 1804, to their art's possibility [a little 'short' possibly of what Riemann, Melville and Whitman could do, 1854].—

I'll confess in fact my surprise—and obvious delight, obviously— to discover tonight even, what I had not somehow or other just got clear, that the date of his 1st Webster is by the Lord of Creation <u>1828</u>.

So if anything goes in a run to expose the general world ignorance or pseudo morphism of what really did go on in the 19th century to produce us—that stupid liberal-existential relativism all lives are now lived on personally & socially, <u>evolution</u> (1809-1882) [that mediocre anthropology which leaves out exactly the other half we need as we turn & that fool Dane of non-action <u>Kierkegaard</u> [1813-1855] <u>in belief</u> by action & production in our lives [& hamper Peirce's perfect geological survey!] the Muslim spectre now is ourself—!

'Tis the 50ish years I wanted to run like a newsreel in front of your eyes: [I do it with a quote, from you know who]:

"Until the discovery of the non-Euclidean geometries [Lobachevsky, 1826 & 1st published 1829, János Bolyai, 1st thought 1823 & 1st published 1832] [& both unknown & unnoticed except for Gauss, almost immediately, himself even concluding in 1830 and coming home into real development & future with B. Riemann, 1854], <u>geometry was universally considered as being exclusively the science of existent space</u>. 11th Edition, VII, opening words, p. 730. Signed A.N.W. (Alfred North Whitehead) *Encyclopedia Britannica,* Geometry section.

And then there was—

So—happily, I hope, for you,

Yrs, now AM October 1, 1-9-6-8

If my use of dates especially birth-dates does seem over-emphatic, you do know the Spenglerism I am backing up to [the one Joe Dunn taught me at Black Mt., I believe it was about the 1st or maybe that 3rd of the group on the Special or Serial View of History I haven't yet mailed off to you.

He sd Spengler says <u>a man's life is an act of giving form to the condition or state of reality</u> [concerned obviously as a moving thing himself] <u>at the exact moment of his birth</u>. So therefore error or truth in the execution of that imperative is the whole shot! Posted off to you:

Oct. 1, 1968

Dear Charles,

What great letters! The matter of the dates—I didn't know about Crazy Horse and only, you say, 28. Thank you. This greatly amplifies for me what I found you first suggesting in "The House for Cpt. John Somes." As a sort of "2nd Half," would you consider letting us publish your Essay on the Matter of, in our Portents series? We pay a little—$25—and Sam has some interesting ideas for designing it. Perhaps an edition of 500 copies, for sale cheap (Eigner's priced at $1: we split on the "collectors' market.") Whatever you say. . . .

We saw the Wilbert Snow record around in Boston in 1961 & didn't get it—too broke—& now to learn you wrote the notes—double damn!! There is of course much more to this dates matter, but let me reflect before I speak—& ask you.

If you already mailed the Special View of History, the mails must have failed you because it hasn't yet arrived—& I do so wish it would! I don't want to mess around in Butterick's <u>previously</u> agreed upon "territory"—your 1965 Pleistocene letters to Jack Clarke I never even heard of—but my glimpses of the Black Mountain College material looked so good they immediately suggested a natural book, dependent as you say on editing. Reading the series whole does interest me—& I will watch the mails closely.

Very busy at various small things. My little girl is becoming so lively & beautiful, a golden age. Sam's off himself for a week or two in the desert, Arizona I think. We wonder if you'll still be in Gloucester the weekend of Nov. 9th. No school on Nov. 11th & we could come see you, maybe with the *Affinity* book (I've pinched Hawley).

Love,
Annie

P.S. Where's the new *Maximus* at? Perfect fall weather to be awaiting new books.

Sunday, October—5th [[1968]]

Dear Annie,

Delighted, if you are, and Sam will enjoy designing it, to have
<u>Portents</u> publish the "Letter, in the Matter of"

—and the only further question wld be those epigraph notes of
Adams? Do you feel they do anything to <u>add</u> to the shot as it stood?
Only if so then let us retain them—& if so we better, one of us, ask
Duncan for the right to lift them from his *Passages*.

I've been a little delayed, the last few days—but I had the loveliest
short visit over Friday night, from my daughter: and what of course did
she see, very deliciously enjoy and ask for—so now I have none—was
the "poster" announcement [of your book]

—actually it was the photo—I mean the whole expanse wowed—
which moved her [Do, by the way, when you get in touch with Hawley,
ask him to get me a few of those, wld you?

Quickly, & back soon,

Charles

Nice to hear of your baby, & yourself—And please keep me on. [Also
will still try to manage to get off to you those enormous "pages."! O

[[28 Fort Square, Gloucester, Mass.]]
1968
Wednesday October 9th

My dear Annie—

Wld love to give that crazy protestant letter of yrs an adequate answer, especially as I do think I gave you an advantage one ought never to: in going further than, the Letter in the Matter of. I was in fact showing you the back of my mind instead that is of simply laying out the hand as such, as I had.

10/9/68

Charles—

Yes, great—Portents will print! I'll write Duncan for the right to quote from *Passages*.

Have asked Hawley for more announcements—& here's 1 for you in the meantime. I said, haven't I, that this photo will be the book's dustwrapper?

We came upon some little magazines that had your stuff, like *Quixote* & *Mag. Of Further Studies* #5—Good things. . . . I am thinking again, & will write.

Love,
Annie

Am very pleased your daughter liked the <u>expanse</u> [in the dustwrapper photograph].

[[Envelope postmarked Gloucester, Mass.
Oct. 11, 1968]]

Dear Annie,

Maybe so though I don't think your stricture applies to the Letter, on the Matter of—and that certainly was the least of it.

That is, the writing does count—and one knows it both as such and when one does it. —Anything in fact in the order of thought—at least, <u>was</u> done under the instruction or order of the <u>muses</u> which is at least what their Father, poets, and—they say—princes or rulers equally had better be:

My muse <u>myoos</u> is <u>kleos</u> & I was particularly delighted today to note Havelock saying in so many words <u>kleos</u> is the equivalent of <u>doxa</u> & then he goes on flatly to say (sentence): "Saga by definition was a celebration of <u>kleos</u>"!

> This, to catch you back (as I go piling it
> along
> O

Thursday October 10th The Mt. must have been in

full regalia! Tropaic Mountain!! OVER

Just to get you off the hook, though, yrself—if on 2nd thoughts you'd <u>think</u> twice abt publishing my original 'Argument' to you. Don't hesitate: I want us always to be on the <u>firmest</u> possible ground!

Love
O

PS [Start here—read after enclosed letter]

Keats knocks me out in the sense that in his letters to Fannie he is always referring to his work—what he aint telling her about—as <u>abstract</u>! And exactly this is what Plato thinks poetry ain't. Therefore he, Plato, calls it <u>doxa</u>! Or, opinion: "state of mind." Secondary. The Muses however say in so many words, it is their Father's <u>mind</u>. They exist to cause to help him with—& <u>kleos is my muse in particular</u>.

Oct. 14, 1968

Dear Charles,

Of course I—Portents—must print your Letter on the Matter of—only the firmest possible ground, always, & no one's ever seen me backtrack. What I wrote you in no way subtracts from your <u>use</u> of history, which of course is the only thing that counts. I am so disgusted & confused about the current American muddle—& withal so <u>uninvolved</u>—the only thing that does hang together is my own work, like on the *Affinity*. But like Cunningham's metaphor about the balance forever being off when the weight wasn't placed right at the beginning on the outside of the foot—and as you wrote in "The House for Cpt. Somes," the only movement left now isn't across but through—& it was this <u>through</u> I was groping for—however one does it. It was a grope (sorry, Ed Sanders), not a gripe—anyway, such fleeting responses should have been spoken aloud, not written down to occupy more space than they were intended for.

I certainly am honored to have had an Olson piece written for me—I don't know if I've said this—& we are very excited that you would let us publish it. I'm enclosing token payment for publication, hoping this won't in any way seem to impinge on the spirit of our friendship. Also included is a transcript of the entire "Matter"—if you could find a moment to check its accuracy, & return it, Sam will begin the design. Then I'll write Duncan about using "Passages 32."

The mountain upstate two weekends ago was beautifully gold &

red. I figure the baby must have covered half a mile, the dog fifty-five. Best of all, I managed photos for the Melville Box (Portents 13 this winter. You'll be 12). Which reminds me—you mentioned in your M.A. thesis you knew about more unsigned Melville appearances (early reviews?) but weren't permitted in 1932 to list them in your bibliography. Have they been revealed since? Why is it I must end on a question, nearly every time?

Love,
Annie

[[90 State Street, Brooklyn Heights, N.Y.]]
Oct. 21, 1968

Dear Charles,

Here are a few more of Hawley's (mis-spelt) advertisements. Sam's in Berkeley this week recording Country Joe, so I expect I'll hear how the book is coming along—& how matters stand with Oyez—very soon.

Just now I'm working on the Melville box getting blow-ups of contemporary material about him in the Berkshire papers, mostly things I uncovered in Pittsfield four summers ago. "Miss Melville Embroiders," farm land for sale, notices of a new book, a lecture, etc. Bits & pieces adding up as I hoped they would. There's still the ultimate personal mystery, but—I don't know why—there's also an inherent power, a sense of life, in the things themselves. There'll also be 4 lines, a quatrain, of an unpublished Melville poem, not good lines, but as you once said, every scrap counts. My other winter's project (it'll take longer than the Melville box), the small press research, moves slowly, as the spirit dictates—which will be more often as the weather gets colder & libraries seem more like the place to be.

I'm looking forward to reading the new *Maximus* book—out soon? Despite the political vaudeville, there are still good things in the wind these days.

Love,
Annie

[[90 State Street, Brooklyn Heights, N.Y.]]
Nov. 3, 1968

Dear Charles

Thought perhaps you could use an extra copy of *The New York Times* review last week—I was very pleased to see it, after all this time!

Hope you are well—turning into winter here, with colds for the baby and wet paws for the dog. Hawley now thinks the *Affinity* book'll be out in mid-December. Graham Mackintosh forgot to send it to the printer. . . .

Love,
Annie

My dear Annie—

Many thanks for sending me both the announcement of the
Mayan show—[Good for Guatemala!]—and for the Rosenthal review
(which I had only seen yesterday, in Brown's book dept., and read, at
Brown's dept. store lunch counter!

I apologize for not getting back to you either the text of the
"Letter" as such—or the huge bundle of the two 1950s "books," the
Lectures on Pleistocene and the Special or Serial View of History. In
the latter case it is discouragement with my present housekeeper, to
do either the mailing or the Xerox right—[and I myself have been in-
bound by the worst bronchitis yet]—

And in the other, the Letter, I am notorious in not being able to
look backward: and without my original I wldn't know how to check
it.

Why don't we—because I am still working up a vertical wall, to
get back & out into just such matters—trust your ability to read my
handwriting (as well as to trust my spacings] - - - - and only where you
have a real doubt, send me both the passage and either the original or a
Xerox of the line or word in doubt?

I think it's better, and wld be sure not to hold things up [even if
Oyez-Mackintosh have, in that instance; damn it.

Also, don't either you or Sam (or the baby) think I wldn't welcome that visit you proposed: My reluctance is solely <u>fear</u> my present health [due only God damn it to completely unsuccessful living circumstances] aren't to be trusted—despite the fact a visit cheers the hell out of me. (I also have delayed to say this, still thinking of some way to get out of here fast, before the cold comes (over)

and into some clime which I don't have to fight—<u>yet</u> (as you'd particularly know) this <u>pit</u> [of hell, even though] is my onlie known survival kit. So I <u>don't</u> want to wander the Earth either!

All right, quickly, & scratchily,

love,
Charles

[[90 State Street, Brooklyn Heights, N.Y.]]
Nov. 18, 1968

Dear Charles,

We tried to get up to see you Nov. 10th—my birthday weekend—
but we phoned & phoned, & when we couldn't reach you, decided not
to risk it. I hope you weren't laid low with bronchitis—such a painful
business! We don't live that much closer than you do to Florida or
California, but we have a cheerful southern exposure & we'd love to
have you visit us for a few days, if only as a chance to get away. One
reason I was sorry we didn't see you on the 10th was that we were going
to offer to drive you back to N.Y. the next day to see Creeley, who was
at the Gotham Book Mart celebrating his book with Robert Indiana.
Damn, all around.

We'll do as you suggest on the transcript of the "Argument"—
unless I have a specific question—& I don't think there are any—we'll
go ahead on my transcription. Right now it'll probably be Portents
#14. #11 is just out, two copies enclosed. Do you remember the letter?
John [[Wieners]] had kept a carbon of it & liked the idea of having it
printed.

Sam just got back from his trip to the Hopi mesas, which he
found very exciting. We're going back together in January for a couple
of weeks (if not before, to ask political asylum. . . .) Their mythology
brings Emerson & Thoreau strangely to mind, but not Melville. What
you wrote in *Ishmael* about his Christianity—he never shook it, not

a spiritual break-through, rather a Western mind. With luck we'll get together someday to talk about the Indians.

We're going to try to get away the weekend after Thanksgiving (Nov. 29/30)—we'll call, & really hope to reach you this time. Be well—

Love, Annie

90 State
B'lyn 11201
[postmarked] 24 Dec 1968

Charles Olson
28 Fort Square
Gloucester, Mass.
[Christmas Card, 1968]

Kraken? Merry Xmas '68,

Annie Sam Mallay

Charters

WESTERN UNION TELEGRAM
DEC 24 1968

ANN AND SAM CHARTERS

90 STATE ST   BROOKLYN HTS   NY

HAM DELICIOUS AND TELL MALLAY TOO STOP
COULDN'T FONE YOU NOT HAVING NUMBER LOVE
AND MERRY CHRISTMAS

CHARLES

[[90 State Street, Brooklyn Heights, N.Y.]]
Jan. 6, 1969

Charles—

The book's here—paperbound copies anyway, hardbound
in another month. I wanted to <u>drive</u> a copy to you in Gloucester
immediately after I'd unwrapped Hawley's package Saturday
afternoon—this not possible, I read it again & thought of you all
weekend. I don't know what you'll think about *Olson/Melville:
A Study in Affinity.* As Peter Howard in Berkeley told you, it isn't
uncritical at times. If you are offended, I hope you will not think I've
presumed upon your total warmth & generosity to me in Melville
matters this past year. I wouldn't have felt I understood the affinity
without your help, & I certainly badgered you with thoughts &
questions throughout. You are the man on earth living closest to
Melville—a fact that holds me fast.

It won't do, a long letter now about how I feel. The book's the
letter to you, of course.

Love—it's self-evident—
Ann Charters

P.S. Hawley's sending you 10 or 20 copies surface mail. Here are 2—
could you possibly read & comment in the <u>unsigned</u> one & return it to
me? I'd like so much to get your reactions, & I can't place myself at 28
Fort Square as you read this time.

WESTERN UNION TELEGRAM   JAN 28 1969

ANN CHARTERS

90 STATE ST   BROOKLYN HEIGHTS NY

DON'T MIND. SIMPLY BOTH SOUTH EXECRATED AND
ININDATED THREE LONG QEEKS. COME UP FROM
IT TODAY AND TO THANK YOU. BOOKS SPREADING
LIKE WILDFIRE. MOST PERSONABLE THING POSSIBLE
EVERYONE ENJOYING IT AND I OF COURSE SIMPLY
RAKING IT ALL IN ON BOTH OUR BEHALFS. WILL
WRITE AS SOON AS POSSIBLE.

CHARLES

[[90 State Street, Brooklyn Heights, N.Y.]]
Feb. 24, 1969

Dear Charles,

Just a note to thank you for the telegram. It was over a month ago
& I should have replied much sooner—but I was in Los Angeles & am
only now getting back to <u>this</u> life in Brooklyn. Floods in California,
walls of snow here, somehow has made for dislocation. Somehow
restful & totally agreeable for February, I think . . . but must work in
March, like the bulbs.

I hear from local stores that the *Affinity* book is moving well, &
Hawley has said he's already getting re-orders. The hardcover edition
is ready, but the dust-jackets are not. This should soon be remedied.
Creeley, Duncan, & Meltzer have told us they like the book—but most
important, <u>you</u> do. I'm so glad—I want to do the 2nd one with the
BMC folders you lent me, a little book now beginning to take shape
in my mind. I'm still hoping to see your comments on the *Affinity*
in the extra copy I sent (I hope Hawley's sent you many more copies;
hardcovers coming too). Robert is coming East for 6 weeks on March
15th, for the N.Y.C. book fair & scouting—

The last few nights Sam & I have been readying the Melville Box
material for production. I finally, after months of tries, got the essay
for it right. It's been too long since I've had a letter from you—I hope
everything is all right, & that you weren't overcome by the snow.

Love,

Annie

P.S. Did you ever cash the Oct. '68 Portents $25 check? It hasn't shown up on the bank statement yet.

[[Olson's note scribbled beside this Postscript: Probably Not—But will!]]

[[28 Fort Square, Gloucester, Mass.]]
Sunday March 2 [[1969]]

Annie,

I think you make me too metaphysical—and I miss terribly that
later shot of yours, about the <u>composition</u> of *Ishmael* [that whole
thing we struck in what, now, must have been abt my last letter to you
(strictly answering yr 'thousand questions')

But it doesn't matter. For the book is itself a new genre—and
my neighbors (as well as Peter who saw, like a shot, the nature of yr
photograph of the Fisherman's Institute—everybody's enjoying it
[including me

Love to yr darling child & to Sam. (Harrassed, as probably now
forever, per usual—no help in sight. So don't therefore mind gaps—or
using yr own letter for my response. Please let me hear from you <u>more
often</u>.

Charles

[[This letter is written on the back of my February 24, 1969, letter.
On the envelope postmarked March 9, 1969, Olson has written the
following:]]

<u>You will note that the accompanying letter has been sitting here
waiting to be mailed for days</u>!

28 Fort Square, Gloucester, Mass.

Friday March 7th—1969

Annie

Let me try to make it another winter (just for the sport of it, and to acknowledge the bound copy in today [which, curiously, feels & looks so differently . . . or I am, between January [9th?] and March 7th. —(The "Introduction" reads marvelously, again.)

Let me start, actually, p. 29. I think, there, you run over like in a traffic accident the book of the law of the blood. That is, as I warned you, drop the Freud. (It deserves as much concern, and attention, as sadism-masochism does [in the term of growing contemporary event— what I think "wrongly" Duncan in his newest book [in yesterday], *The Truth and Life of Myth,* calls like, myth is psychosis—example, clearly, Sirhan. Prose-wise, syntactically, Sirhan is psyche.

There is that edge of difference between murdering the Father and cannibalism. One in fact is survival [why Captain Porter's action forming the lots has such lameness in it: authority yielded to equality)—What I was talking about in "Moses" is different from the Essex narrative ----- or I'd not have treated them apart: creatively, one does not repeat.

Though it is true [as Havelock, alone, of living men—or anybody possibly since the Areopagian court, maybe] that the laws themselves— that is, law as an invention & principle—does mean [as nomoi, nomos] . . .

The fact that Hesiod was the first to use it is tantamount to who I want you to know as of myself as not the philosopher-poet & Emersonian you have in the text: the mythological—and again, you are not as handy with Maximus as with my more written [& not philosophical, reductive, analytical, informational] pieces—

I'm only asking you to tie yourself up in knots—better, leave the knots to be tied up until one can find out how to untie [or, as in the classic arrogant case, cut 'em]

"Nomos wld describe, as it does in Hesiod, the universal law of hard work or the prohibition instinctively obscured by mankind against cannibalism."

The book of the law of the blood was in fact the Globe massacre, not the Essex story.

I hope you will welcome any such letters after the fact as I think you had before. Collect them, in case I shld do more. This matter is a real one to me [as I took pains to worry you, June 4th or 5th, not to get into that Freud thing.]

Yrs in the saddle

O

(PS: I just checked the Moses passage, & I see the sentence [It is cannibalism] which must have mislead you. If you read the para. through you'll see it's the Father—or Nature—who satisfies—and we rebel [against the Law: Give us this Day our Daily Bread!] The inversion of the <u>Essex</u> is the <u>Globe:</u> the Whale is King of Cannibals. In spelling out or as I say summing one of the chosen Facts into the Book on the Other you denude the critical opposites of the Phantom in the seas of life. Or the shark-infested sea [Keats]. And hombres & feminores

PS2 beyond this point you do not go—the bound-ary

I also by the way take exception—and I think you muddle, by getting into it at all—the damned existing biz [which Creeley, happily, in that Introduction, by posing it directly vis-à-vis Camus, got it straight: I can't find the passage now, but you will know where it is: my dogmatism has nothing to do with the modern carousel of multiple: if—again!—you had read the Maximus with the same confidence you had this other book—you'd be more justified than to call me dogmatic or those who do like Duncan) <u>gnostic.</u>

Oh yes, I found it. P. 19: You shld examine the matter of impetus.

Or be altogether exact here [and absolutely Dead-Eye Dick to that fucking modern Wraith, multiplicity]: "The widest group of automorphisms one can possibly envisage for a continuum consists of all continuous transformations; the corresponding Geometry is called Topology. Topology is not a philosophy. It is a measurement system of forms, and is thus properly a geometry!"

[[90 State Street, Brooklyn Heights, N.Y.]]
April 10, 1969

Dear Charles,

Sorry, sorry to have waited so long to reply. Hit here by the tail end of winter's coughs, colds, aches & wheezes—and final work on the Melville Box. Some of its out-growth enclosed, and when the cardboard box for the construct and the 25 tape copies are in, you'll have #1/25. The pamphlet "Melville in the Berkshires" will be in the box, but is also being sold separately. We got finished sheets and photographs from the printers last night, and lay them out and listened to your reading [[of the poem "Letter for Melville 1951"]] at the same time. Your voice is the perfect other-dimension of the visual construct, and the objects themselves gave back to your poem a wonderful Berkshire <u>presence</u>, an unexpected reflection that delighted me.

Thank you for the long letter going over the *Affinity* book in such critical detail. It was illuminating, and it doesn't tie me in knots, since the pen is mightier than the sword (that cuts through Nots). I just hope you find the defects and shortcomings and blind alleys less bothersome than the achievement—if you feel there is one. I liked best your saying the book is itself a new genre, because I tried, you see. I really learned from your experience, took whole your perception that criticism must be a creative act. That's why, among other things, the photographs.

If you still want me to work on another Oyez book, using the BMC material, I'd like to do one, perhaps 50-60 pages, with "The Special View of History" as center. I'd write an intro, and ask Duncan and Dorn if they'd like to contribute something on what they remember of being with you there. My idea of this book is to follow a pencil outline of the "History" seminar I found in one of the folders; along the lines of

THE CONTENTS (the note by way of prefaces, intro., or summary)

THE STANCE (invocation on history)

THE VIEW (in two parts)

    THE METRICAL

        1. The 4 Objects/Subjects

        2. The 4 Factors

        3. The 4 Qualities

    & THE TOPOLOGICAL

        1. Cosmos

        2. Muthos

Going through the folders, I think I've assembled most of the contents, with some additional notes Wieners furnished. There might also be a chart or two, a reading list, some loose notes that you used to get into the lectures, etc. Whatever you'd like too. If you want such a book, let me know soon—for then I'll type out what I have and send it to you for going-over.

Last spring, my crocuses and hyacinths were flowering with our Melville letters. It's a great pleasure going on.

Love,

Annie

P.S. Into *Maximus 4,5,6*—so great & beautiful, Charles

June 23, 1969

Dear Charles,

Okay, okay, our phone talk last night did it—24 hours later (& my San Francisco trip well in the back of my mind), the questions are upon you:

The book will probably be titled something like

OLSON AT BLACK MOUNTAIN

"The Special View of History"   so—

1. Where can I find out the details of your association with the school, dates you were there, courses taught, duties assumed, etc? If nothing is published, could you fill me in on when you first came to BMC, what you thought of the place, what concepts you had about education you wished to explore there, etc. etc. whatever seems pertinent to you.

2. Did you ever, in Spring '56, actually present "The Special View" to BMC students? I mean, Duncan doesn't recall you ever lectured from typed lecture notes. He said the classes were seminars, discussion groups. Yet from your folder of notes it's obvious that you worked hard on "The Special View"—with prepared reading assignments, diagrams, weekly presentations. But were these ever used in class?

3. Duncan, Don Allen & I all have Wieners' notes on "The Special View"—they're a large part (but not all) of my material, in fact. But they read like your prose, not his lectures notes. What were they,

please? Did Wieners work with you on them?

4. In conceiving "The Special View," did you have in mind any type of student—one interested in writing and the arts, certainly—but was it part of an actual writing course?

5. Did you present the lectures in San Francisco the following fall of '56? McClure, for example, remembered you about that time speaking to a group of people at his apartment—did it involve "The Special View"? If so, do you recall any of the other people there?

If you wish, your answers to these questions will be sort of like an up-dating of the lectures—so any other comments on the material and your BMC experience are very welcome. Please answer soon, Charles, before the weather turns hot and you don't want to think back about what you were doing so long ago. I've written Creeley, and if it's also all right with him (I'd like to talk with him about his association with you and BMC), I'll be up July 7th.

But hoping to hear from you long before then . . .

Love,
Annie

I came with no ideas. Black Mt. did it all. Whatever those notes of John's are, I suspect they are either Gerald Van dee Wisles' or possibly Joe Dunne's.

As I told you, one long summary sheet on pink paper was something Duncan mimeographed as a repeat in 5 evenings lasting about 3 hours in Feb-March 1957 San Francisco: McClure and Duncan's Jess another evening Madeline Gleason's—& others presenting that poetess . . . Jack Spicer Mike Rumaker Phil Whalen Tom Parkinson one evening at the home of another of the 'Maidens'— also Jim Broughton etc.

1st Black Mt fall 1948, & visited once a month, for a week, for the rest of the year; then for summer session fall 1949

Lectured & read one night in like May 1950

Returned summer session 1951. Ended up there 1951-closing fall 1956 & on for another yr to settle its affairs, until 1 July 1957. [Cut out, fall 1952; also cut out, winter 1955-6

What you have were used—very much so. Duncan's memory is faulty.

Ok See ya then happily on such a funny date.

Charles (Fri. June 27th—1-9-6-9

117

Wld advise <u>very strongly</u> at calling this anything but a vision of history ---- Other, & a wholly different aspect, actually me at that place. --- Many more business & persons etc.

[[On back of envelope]]

PS 1 Did I write Richard Duerden in list as well as Jess & Mike of course—there were 25 all told, @ $5 a head (for 5)

PS 2 It was the week following my reading at the San Francisco Art Museum (or part of the Poetry Center's Program there that year)

PS3 Also read for Jeanne D'Orge over the weekend session at the Cherry Theater in Carmel

PS4 We were the guests while in San Francisco of Ruth Witt-Diamant

PS5 I read at Berkeley (for Tom Parkinson's class) & in the front row, unbeknownst to me, were the two leading poetesses of the class: Diane Wakoski & Lady Panna de Cholnuke [I am the godfather of her newest boy]

PS6 3rd house was on Telegraph Hill . . .

[[90 State Street, Brooklyn Heights, N.Y.]]
July 8, 1969—just gotten back from
Gloucester

Charles—

Thanks for the Melville celebration—to have read the *Globe*
review—the 1st ever—of the/my book in your house, will never be
forgotten. Also the talk by the water, the beautiful celebratory dinner,
the Janis Joplin-type waitress episode of the spilled sour cream—not
to mention giving you the Melville construct & photograph blown-up
face, eyes radiating from your bookshelves through to your kitchen
---etc. etc. etc. Thank you!

About *The Special View of History*—only, now, to return your two-
page outline, that I've just finished copying.

More later, as the lady said.
Annie

JULY 10 69 GLOUCESTER MASS

ANN CHARTERS

    90 STATE ST   BROOKLYN NY

JUST CHANGE THE WORD CRUCIAL TO NEXAL AND
SEND IT OFF. GOOD LUCK AND HAPPY VOYAGE. LOVE,

    CHARLES

[[90 State Street, Brooklyn Heights, N.Y.]]
July 13, 1969

Charles—

Your telegram sent me reeling—

The word change has been made, & all the rest is up to Hawley and his Merrie Men in California.

Did Melville's photograph smile on your bookshelf as you dictated the telegram? Knowing how happy I'd be? And how <u>right</u> it was? I think I understand a little the difficulty you had deciding what to do—& I am very honored you said yes, after all.

Gotham Book Mart is out of the paperback Cape—but here's their last copy of the hard cover edition. And I've asked Hawley to send you ten *Affinity* books. Maybe you could show one to the German shepherd that bit me Tuesday—so I'll be more cordially welcomed back to the Fort.

Love you, Charles—& I <u>am</u> honored.
Annie

Dear Charles,

Wet overcast days here, but my mood is still flying high with your telegram go-ahead and, more recently, the moonmen adventure. Does the current space exploration and setting foot on land unknown have any of the quality of excitement that was in the world 300 years ago when America was being moved in on, I wonder? My Russian grandmother once said that she'd have been an astronaut if she'd been born at the right time—which was right in character for a lady who'd moved west across the Atlantic in her own adventure over half a century ago. I'd go with her, of course. Maybe Mallay really will, although she seems to be too happy where she is. (Not _too_ happy, happy.)

Could you tell me two more things about history? (1) Transcribing Creeley's tape, I remembered he'd told me that in a trolley car in Majorca long ago, Duncan once leaned over to him and said, "You're not interested in history, are you?" Creeley said he agreed readily at the time, but he's not at all sure now just what he agreed to. Do you know? (Wow, how this trolley rattles in time!) And (2), the word "nexal" having been inserted as you requested—don't you think that kids today _are_, many of them, living the concept of history you described at Black Mountain? How do you see it reified ten or so years later?

I sent a copy of the *Boston Globe* Olson review onto Hawley, and he wrote back "Thanks. #1 yes—but 'review'?" But in a recent little magazine *Works*, Alan Brilliant (he of the Santa Barbara package, Unicorn Press, that arrived when I was with you), wrote "In the United States, Oyez has been, consistently, the model press." Small cheers for our side.

We bought a papercover *Maximus, IV, V, VI,* in Brentano's, a stack of them there a week ago, Grossman $3.95. I assume you know about this, although you mentioned trouble with the American edition, and Bob Wilson said it was being recalled for its errors in photo-offsetting. Who in America, Charles, will bring out the great edition of all the Maximus to date? Such a great sweep and depth it would have, and a much bigger audience for your work.

We're hoping to bring Mallay swimming off the Fort at the end of August, but I'd like to hear from you on the history matter before that, if you've time. How's the essay going you began in the kitchen during our morning rap? So many provocative notions!

Annie: Answer to Question #1:

The trolley-car then is the 'history'

Like the RED SEA was the suf or Pagoon Serbonis [on today's
maps the Sebcha el Bardawil] which was dried out for 30 minutes to
one hour by the tsunami from the explosion which blew Atlantis into
the sea (for which Atlantis read Thera]

& 600 not 600,000 Hebrews passed before the re-wash of the
tsunami caught the Egyptian army & the Pharoh

Not too long for a trolley car made of such twones as the Twa'
Roberts especially in sometime about what—Barcelona 1955?

Answer, Question #2:

History is whatever happens & if it is significant enough to
be recorded the amt. of time of the event can be <u>minute</u>! [example,
previous incident—I don't mean the Jews, & Moses alone, I mean the
Twa'Roberts, Barcelona, etc.—<u>trolley-car</u>]

Yrs with love & continuing success— &
approbation,
Charles

[[On the back of the envelope]]

[Wed. 2 PM July 30th]

PS: My daughter right at this moment is looking at the [[Melville]] Box—& as a lover of Salem, and of Hawthorne, as well as . . . just sd she thinks yr Box is "great"!

And she's <u>not</u> a flatterer!

Charles

Friday September 12th 1969

[[postcard with a 1957 view of *Mayflower II*]]

Just for your cogitation:

G. Bachelard, *La poétique de l'espace* (Paris, 1958)

I mean of course the title. Don't know myself [as usual] the book.

O.

Sept. 29, 1969

Dear Charles,

Some things for you—but I wish I were delivering them! I tried to arrange a trip to see you two weeks ago, but it didn't work out—then your Pilgrim ship postcard & I began to look for that Bachelard book. Found it yesterday, staring no winking at me on the other side of the Gotham Book Mart's window, translated which looks like a very good thing.

Also a new Portents, enclosed. Sam drew the illustrations, possibly motivated by the illustrated magazines we leafed through searching for older periodicals to include in the Melville construct.

How are you? I hope well. Mallay Charters yearns to wade in the water off the Fort, like her hard-working mother.

Love,
Annie

Cressey Beach at Stage Fort Park, Gloucester, Mass.

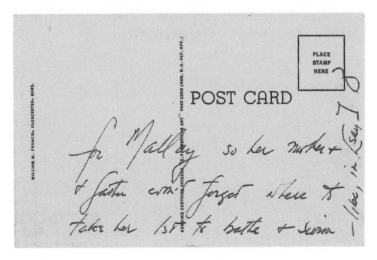

[[Tinted postcard of Cressey Beach at Stage Fort Park, Gloucester, Mass.]]

[[in blue ink]]

For Mallay so her mother &

& father won't forget where to

take her 1st to bathe & swim

—like, in [say]

O

Italian Fishing Boats, Gloucester, Mass.

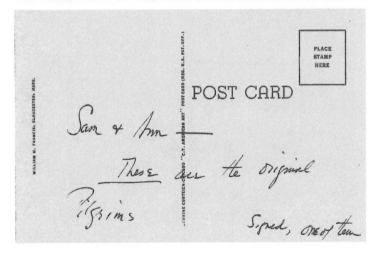

POST CARD

PLACE
STAMP
HERE

WILLIAM H. FRANCIS, GLOUCESTER, MASS.

"GENUINE CURTEICH-CHICAGO "C.T. AMERICAN ART" POST CARD (REG. U.S. PAT. OFF.)

Sam & Ann

These are the original

Pilgrims

Signed, one of ten

[Tinted postcard of Italian Fishing Boats, Gloucester, Mass.]

[In blue ink]

Sam & Ann –

<u>These</u> are the original Pilgrims.

Signed, one of them

Charles Olson in Gloucester
Summer 1968

A photo essay by Ann Charters

My shore, my sounds, my earth, my place, afterwards, in between, and since

In the land of plenty, have
nothing to do with it
                        take the way of
the lowest,
including
your legs, go
contrary, go

sing

28 Fort Square, where Olson had his apartment

What kills me is, how do these others think
the eyes are
sharp? by gift? bah   by love of self? try it   by god? ask
the bean sandwich

There are no hierarchies, no infinite, no such many as mass,
                                              there are only
eyes in all heads,
to be looked out of

Door to Olson's second-floor apartment, right of stairs

Looking through the window into Olson's kitchen

I count the blessings, the leak in the faucet
which makes of the sink time, the drop
of the water on water as sweet
as the Seth Thomas
in the old kitchen
my father stood in his drawers to wind (always
he forgot the 30th day, as I don't want to remember
the rent

That's
the combination the ocean
out one window rolling
100 yards from me, the City
out the door on the next quarter up a hill was a dune
300 years covered very little so that, a few years back
a street crew were and I picked up the white
sand

On my back the
Harbor and over it the long arm'd shield of Eastern
point. Wherever I turn or look in whatever direction,
and near me, on any quarter, all possible combinations of
Creation . . . .

Main Street
Is deserted, the hills
are bull-dozed
away. The River alone,
and Stage Fort Park
where the Merrimac
once emptied under the ice
to the Banks survive

Said Mrs. Tarantino,
occupying the yellow house
on fort constructed like
a blockhouse said
You have a long nose, meaning
you stick it into every other person's
business, do you not? And I couldn't
say anything
but that I
do

Charles Olson and George Butterick

I would be an historian as Herodotus was, looking
for oneself for the evidence of
what is said: Altham says
Winslow
was at Cape Ann in April,
1624

. . . . Stage Fort is
what Babson called it, the only hundred acres
on this cape could possibly have fit the foolish hope
of Somerset and Dorset men to do on this rock coast
what England might have thought New England might be

It is undone business
I speak of, this morning,
with the sea
stretching out
from my feet

In an outgoing tide
Of the Annisquam River, each summer, at the August full,
they throw flowers, which, from the current there, at the Cut,
reach the harbor channel, and go

these bouquets (there are few, Gloucester, who can afford florists' prices)

float out
                    you can watch them go out into,
the Atlantic

Dogtown is soft
in every season
high up on her granite
horst, light growth
of all trees and bushes
strong like a puddle's ice

blossoming apple trees
in the Paradise of Dogtown
in the spring   crabbed apples

dried out apples   apples as dry
as thorns   boughs of apple trees
to write with as a swatch grabbed off
at the writing table in the whole outdoors

                    Dogtown to the right the ocean
to the left
                    opens out the light   the river flowing
at my feet
                    Gloucester to my back
          the light hangs
          from the wheel of heaven
                              the great Ocean
                    in balance
                              the air is as wide as the light

one loves only form,
and form only comes
into existence when
the thing is born.

my memory is
the history of time

An American
Is a complex of occasions,
themselves a geometry
of spatial nature.

I have this sense,
that I am one
with my skin

. . . . . tell you? ha! Who
can tell another how
to manage the swimming?

he was right: people

don't change. They only stand more
revealed. I,
likewise

Note before
"Melville in the Berkshires"

My essay about Melville created for the Portents box "Melville in the Berkshires," referred to in my February 24, 1969, and April 10, 1969, letters to Olson, was a product of my deep immersion in Olson and Melville during the winter of 1969. Listening to John Cage read one of his experimental "cut-up" prose constructs during a Merce Cunningham dance program in New York City in February was the direct stimulus—Olson, Cunningham, and Cage were all inspiring teachers at Black Mountain College. Instead of producing an academic essay like the Columbia University dissertation I had completed a few years earlier on American writers in the Berkshires, I took Olson and Cage as my instructors, writing this new Melville essay in the spirit of their creative freedom and imagination.

Melville in the Berkshires

Ann Charters:

Herman Melville:

with fairest flowers,
Whilst summer lasts, and I live here, Fidele—

I came to the Berkshires looking for Herman Melville. I had
never found him in libraries, and I was determined to come
closer to him than the printed page. Pittsfield, Massachusetts,
the town he had lived in for thirteen years, seemed a good
place to start. I drove there and spent the first night in a tourist
home. The next morning I walked across the street to a faded
yellow frame house that had a painted sign ROOMS in front of
it, and I found the place I lived in for three summers.

When I removed into the country, it was to occupy an old-
fashioned farm-house, which had no piazza—a deficiency the
more regretted, because not only did I like piazzas, as somehow
combining the coziness of indoors with the freedom of outdoors,
and it is so pleasant to inspect your thermometer there, but the
country round was such a picture, that in berry time no boy

climbs hill or crosses vale without coming upon easels planted in every nook, and sun-burnt painters painting there. A very paradise of painters. The circle of the stars cut by the circle of the mountains. At least, so looks it from the house; though, once upon the mountains, no circle of them can you see.

The roominghouse was on West Housatonic Street in Pittsfield, "west" and "housatonic" spiritual landmarks both of my trip and of the particular place. The first summer I stalked the Berkshire streets searching ghosts—besides Melville's, traces of the presence of Hawthorne, Thoreau, Holmes, Longfellow, Bryant, and their contemporaries Fanny Kemble and Catherine Sedgwick, lady writers who also lived in the county over a hundred years before. It was a graduate English student's quest, a sentimentalist's quest, a futile quest. The ghosts had long since left the streets. I put away my maps showing the location of their farmhouses, estates and cottages. I looked into the roominghouse instead.

I introduced myself into Coulter's house on a wet Monday noon (for the snow had thawed) . . . I was struck by the aspect of the room. The house was old, and constitutionally damp. The window-sills had beads of exuded dampness upon them. The shriveled sashes shook in their frames, and the green panes of glass were clouded with the long thaw . . . damp, damp, damp—the heavy atmosphere charged with all sorts of incipiencies—

I found it a quiet place, cool even in the hottest August afternoons, although the frequent thunder showers always keep the Berkshire summer temperatures down. The people there were old, widowed, self-contained, living out the end years of a respectable life, cast out of their children and grandchildren's days for want of space, material and emotional. The Irish wife of a chauffeur who had driven cars on one of the wealthy Lenox estates thirty years before, a gravely polite, meticulously dressed old man who had sold haberdashery on Main Street in Pittsfield for most of his working life. Altogether about half a dozen retired working people. None of them had thought at all about Herman Melville, one of their neighbors.

What grand irregular thunder, thought I, standing on my hearthstone among the Acroceraunian hills, as the scattered bolts boomed overhead, and crashed down among the valleys, every bolt followed by zigzag irradiations, and swift slants of sharp rain, which audibly rang, like a charge of spear-points, on my low shingled room. I suppose though, that the mountains hereabouts break and churn up the thunder, so that it is far more glorious here than on the plain.

The inhabitants of the roominghouse gave me a sense of the way Melville might have lived in his Berkshire time. Every morning, before eight o'clock, I walked to the corner bakery. There was always an old man on the porch as I went out, sitting on one of the painted iron chairs, observing the morning glory vines growing on the worn wooden railing. He always lifted his hat and we exchanged a view on the day's probable weather. I never asked if he had his gaze fastened on the worms that worried Melville in the center of his flowers. From his conversation I merely assumed he was judging the morning dew on the leaves and lawn.

Early one morning in Spring, being too full of hypoes to sleep, I sallied out to walk on my hillside pasture. It was a cool and misty, damp, disagreeable air. The country looked underdone, its raw juices squirting all round. I buttoned out this squitchy air as well as I could with my lean, double-breasted dress-coat—my overcoat being so long-skirted I only used it in my wagon—and spitefully thrusting my crab-stick into the oozy sod, bent my blue form to the steep ascent of the hill . . . beyond, on the mountains, lay light patches of snow, strangely relieved against their russet sides; all the humped hills looked like brindled kine in the shivers. The woods were strewn with dry dead boughs, snapped off by the riotous winds of March . . . I sat down for a moment on a great rotting log nigh the top of the hill, my back to a heavy grove, my face presented toward a wide sweeping circuit of mountains enclosing a rolling, diversified country.

Usually after breakfast, to get the day started, I went to the library. Not to read, but to play the piano. Like Melville, who drove his mother to church on Sundays and waited out the service by sitting in the hotel opposite the park in the center of town reading newspapers.

Presently I was alone, and all was hushed. I laid down my pipe, not feeling exactly tranquil enough now thoroughly to enjoy it. Taking up one of the newspapers, I began, in a nervous, hurried sort of way, to read by the light of a candle placed on a small stand drawn close to the fire. . . . Try as I would, I could not succeed much at reading. Somehow I seemed all ear and no eye.

Around ten, I returned to my room and the books I was working on. The house would be cool and still, the old man gone from the shaded porch to wherever he spent the day. I suspect playing solitaire in his room (once only he left his door partly open around 3 pm, and I passed it in the hall, a hot day. He was inside in his undershirt, his back to the door, straightening something on the top of the bureau). The roominghouse had been used by the landlady first as a private home, where she raised her five children, and the hallways kept the private character, with the dark mahogany woodwork and green carpeted stairs, the rickety tables each with a yellow shaded lamp, a white doily, and a clean glass fluted ashtray, three such identical polished tables, one for each storey, marshalled exactly one above the other on the three floors with the scrubbed linoleum bathrooms alongside them.

Under the apex of the roof was a rude, narrow, decrepit stepladder, something like a Gothic pulpit-stairway, leading to a pulpit-like platform, from which a still narrower ladder—a sort of Jacob's ladder—led some ways higher to the lofty scuttle. . . . The light of the garret came from this sole source, filtrated through a dense curtain of cobwebs. Indeed, the whole stairs, and platform, and ladder, were festooned and carpeted, and canopied with cobwebs.... In these cobwebs swung, as in aerial catacombs, myriads of all tribes of mummied insects.

Inside my room—I closed the door carefully—I made coffee and tried not to stare out the window at the robins and sparrows in the maple tree. They had a lively domestic circle out there that occasioned incredible stretches of songs, gossip, and bursts of movement. The cars rolling down West Housatonic Street a few yards away were oblivious, so must I be. Melville must have listened to the birds in his trees opposite his second storey window, too, perhaps longer than to the chatter of his mother, wife, and sisters in their sewing circle around his large fireplace downstairs.

I planted the chair invitingly on the broad hearth, where a little fire had been kindled that afternoon to dissipate the dampness, not the cold; for it was early in the month of September.

Four or five hours later, I stopped working, changed into a bathing suit and loose sundress, picked up a towel and started off to Lake Onota, about two miles walk away. In the hallway downstairs, large rectangles of sun filtered through the dark, worn screen door; the porch was very warm and totally deserted. Far behind me, deep somewhere in the house, I would hear faint sounds of teacups being rinsed. I guess they napped, or visited, away the afternoon.

A sultry hour, and I wore a light hat, of yellow sinnet, with white duck trousers—both relics of my tropic sea-going. Clogged in the muffling ferns, I softly stumbled, staining the knees a sea-green.

All those hours for myself, to do exactly as I pleased. I thought my simple life more like Thoreau's than Melville's, for Melville lived in the Berkshires surrounded by his family—he came there to live as a young man with a wife and child, and left thirteen years later a middle-aged man with wife and four children, having supported them and his mother and two sisters at various times in his Pittsfield farmhouse, Arrowhead. However our different circumstances, Melville's and mine, we still shared the common fact of geography: I was living in Pittsfield, where he had been, our houses about two miles apart. On days when I didn't feel like swimming, I walked to his old farmhouse or drove my car to local places he had seen and described. I sat in his clover fields, hiked in the mountains he'd had visions about—disquieting visions, since his experiences were so frequently troubled, and he was so often ill. I furtively skirted the mowed grounds of the Pittsfield Country Club, dressed in madras bermudas and a white tee shirt, trying to look like a member, because their golf course led to a wooded stretch of property between the club and Melville's farm, woods and a small lake beside the railroad tracks where I'm sure

Melville walked, and where he rode horseback with his spirited and wealthy neighbor Mrs. Morewood. I visited an old, old lady in Pittsfield, great-grandniece of Mrs. Morewood, who showed me pictures of Melville's friend and a faded handwritten copy of one of her graceful "verses." Did Melville read poetry with her? Or just pay her gallant compliments, and attend—with his wife and children—her fancy dress parties beside the secluded lake? He wisely burned the letters from her before he left Arrowhead. She kept most of his.

On I went. . . . A pasture rose before me. Letting down five mouldering bars—so moistly green, they seemed fished up from some sunken wreck—a wigged old Aries, long-visaged, and with crumpled horn, came snuffing up; and then, retreating, decorously led on along a milky-way of white-weed, past dim-clustering Pleiades and Hyades, of small forget-me-nots; and would have led me further still his astral path, but for golden flights of yellow-birds—pilots, surely, to the golden window, to one side flying before me, from bush to bush, towards deep woods—which woods themselves were luring—and, somehow, lured, too, by their fence, banning a dark road, which, however dark, led up. I pushed through; when Aries, renouncing me now for some lost soul, wheeled, and went his wiser way. Forbidding and forbidden ground—to him.

I also, of course, came to have a feeling for Pittsfield. Evenings I took another walk, after dinner, around the streets near the center of town, not on the outskirts in almost-country, where Arrowhead is only a leap ahead of the subdivision houses crawling closer to its meadows.

There are some strange summer mornings in the country, when he who is but a sojourner from the city shall early walk forth into the fields, and be wonder-smitten with the trance-like aspect of the green and golden world. Not a flower stirs; the trees forget to wave; the grass itself seems to have ceased to grow; and all Nature, as if suddenly become conscious of her own profound mystery, and feeling no refuge from it but silence, sinks into this wonderful and indescribable repose.

Pittsfield's a quiet town with block after block of big old frame houses set solidly on little lawns. Inside the big houses are cellars and attics and two or three floors of spacious rooms. Shuttered porches and dingy gingerbread trim without; white molding, flowered wallpaper, faded carpets within. Inhabitants had larger households in Melville's time. Now the houses are boarded into separate apartments, or rooms for the elderly, or tourists, "guests" like me. Traffic moves patiently on the roads, waiting turns at the lights until all other cars have passed, circling restlessly around the one-way streets in downtown Pittsfield, radios playing. There is really nothing special to do in town. In the darkness, all roads lead out to deserted pizza stands or blacktop shopping centers.

No fence was seen, no enclosure. Near by—ferns, ferns, ferns;
further—woods, woods, woods; beyond—mountains, mountains,
mountains; then—sky, sky, sky. Turned out in aerial commons,
pasture for the mountain moon. Nature, and but nature, house
and all; even a low cross-pile of silver birch, piled openly, to
season; up among whose silvery sticks, as through the fencing of
some sequestered grave, sprang vagrant raspberry bushes—willful
assertors of their right of way.

The nights are very still, in winter very cold. Then the sounds
are inside the rooms, in warm beds, couples huddling for
warmth or love. Making love in Pittsfield has a dark quality
all its own. Dark enough to suggest incest to Melville. The
act connecting with the giants of man's pre-history whom he
imagined writhing on Greylock's stoney sides.

The far summit fairly smoked with frost; white vapors curled
up from its white-wooded top, as from a chimney. The intense
congelation made the whole country look like one petrifaction.
The steel shoes of my pung crunched and gritted over the vitreous,
chippy snow, as if it had been broken glass. . . . Brittle with
excessive frost, many colossal tough-grained maples, snapped in
twain like pipe-stems, cumbered the unfeeling earth. . . . Gusts of
violent wind shrieked through the shivered pass, as if laden with
lost spirits bound to the unhappy world . . . and all but shoved
my high-back pung up-hill. Trees groaned as the fitful gusts
remorselessly swept through them.

I had a vision once on Greylock. The highest mountain in Massachusetts, it's a haunted place, the traces of Melville, Thoreau, Hawthorne, Holmes visible—with a host of other spirits—to those who look. Early one evening in July I took the road to the summit and slept overnight in the car so I'd be there before dawn. Shortly before five in the morning I awoke to thick mist that was solid fog. I made my way to the observatory at the place where Thoreau had awakened to the same clouds a hundred years earlier. He was fortunate; he slept in the top of the observatory and climbed above the clouds. When I was there, things had changed a little. The new tower is locked. Becalmed on the ground, I spread my rubber poncho on the wet earth near some wiry bushes weighted with dew, and sat down to wait. The mist about me was impenetrable. It swirled and drifted and clung in the air so thickly that if night were passing and the sun coming up, it would be hard to tell the moment of dawn. Nearly an hour went by, very quietly. The time by my watch was after sunrise, and still no trace of sun burning through the deep mist. Wrapped in sweaters, a little drowsy, I lay back on the ground, staring upward. The damp wind died down in the stunted trees, and birds began to sing. I peered upward, trying to catch a light shining in the east through the white mist. Suddenly, without warning, the clouds parted directly overhead and I stared up into calm blue sky, up into a world where the sun had been burning unobscured for an hour, an eternity. Nothing but pure blue space, deeper than anything I'd ever looked into before. A space so vast I could

hear it sounding in the distance. A moment there—and the
swirling grey mist covered it over again. It might be half the
morning before it dawned again, or no time at all.

My eye ranged over the capacious rolling country, and over the
mountains, and over the village, and over a farmhouse here and
there, and over woods, groves, streams, rocks, fells—and I thought
to myself, what a slight mark, after all, does man make on this
huge great earth. Yet the earth makes a mark on him.

By the middle of October, the weather gets cold and raw.
Berkshire winters last forever. The spring is slow and cold,
viscous mud under the melting snow in the fields, the earth
reluctantly opening to receive beans and corn and pumpkins,
later flowering idly under the sun into clover and buttercups
and pungent queen anne's lace.

In summer, too, Canute-like, sitting here, one is often reminded of
the sea. For not only do long ground-swells roll the slanting grain,
and little wavelets of the grass ripple over upon the low piazza, as
their beach, and the blown down of dandelions is wafted like the
spray, and the purple of the mountains is just the purple of the
billows, and a still August noon broods upon the deep meadows,
as a calm upon the Line; but the vastness and the lonesomeness
are so oceanic, and the silence and the sameness, too, that the first
peep of a strange house, rising beyond the trees, is for all the world
like spying, on the Barbary coast, an unknown sail.

Melville walked the fields over the same muddy paths I
followed in the upland pasture in back of Arrowhead. Tracks
of a wagon path are still visible in the weeds most of the way
up the hill. To the west, at the top of the hill in back of his
house, beyond the pasture, the corn stalks end at dark pine
woods, where mushrooms grow until the weather turns too
cold. To the east and north, the countryside falls away—open,
elevated, spacious. Greylock in the north, one in the chain of
far-flung, dark mountains floating in clouds away from the
land, dominates the view. It seems very old, distant, remote,
living in another time just as surely as the inhabitants of my
roominghouse on West Housatonic Street. To stand beside
the withered cornstalks—Melville planted them—is to see
what he saw daily when he wrote his books; nothing important
has changed. A circle of clouds and mountains, hints of the
Pittsfield rooftops through the trees, the road past Arrowhead's
meadows, the house and barn, the maples and birches, the
hillside corn and clover, the grasses, ferns, daisies thick
underfoot. The years in Pittsfield left their mark on Melville,
not the other way around. No place more than this Berkshire
hillside brings you closer to him there.

Notes to the Correspondence

AC – January 7, 1968

Lawrence and Dahlberg—Edward Dahlberg (1900-1977) was Olson's early mentor and the author of the literary study *Do These Bones Live* (1941). In 1948 Dahlberg taught briefly at Black Mountain College before Olson's arrival. D.H. Lawrence (1885-1930) wrote *Studies in Classic American Literature* (1923), a classic work of literary criticism that inspired Dahlberg and Olson.

CO – January 10, 1968

Originally, *Call Me Ishmael* was published by Reynal & Hitchcock in New York in 1947. It was reprinted by Grove Press in New York in 1958 and by Jonathan Cape in London in 1966. In 1971 it was published by City Lights in San Francisco in an edition that is still in print. The edition translated into French by Maurice Beerblock as *Appelez-moi Ismaël* was issued by Gallimard in Paris in 1962.

AC – February 12, 1968

The 62-page collection of Olson's early poetry, *In Cold Hell, In Thicket*, was a book designed by Robert Creeley, published at his Divers Press, and issued as #8 (first series) of *Origin* magazine published by Cid Corman in Boston in 1953.

CO – February 14, 1968

During 1942-1945, Olson worked as the assistant chief of the Wartime Office of Facts and Figures in the Office of War Information in Washington, D.C.

AC – March 2, 1968

Charles Olson, "A House Built by Cpt. John Somes 1763" was first published in *A Pamphlet* III, 7 on 12 June 1962. It was reprinted in *Wild Dog* 17 on 8 June 1965.

AC – March 12, 1968

Non-Euclidean proof—More than forty years after I wrote this letter to Olson, I discovered Alex Bellos' book *Alex's Adventures in Numberland: Dispatches from the Wonderful World of Mathematics* (London: Bloomsbury, 2010). Bellos described "Non-Euclidean" geometry as a "watershed for mathematics in that it described a theory of physical space that totally contradicted our experience of the world, and therefore was hard to imagine, but nevertheless contained no mathematical contradictions, and so was as mathematically valid as the Euclidean system that came before" (p. 383). In *The Elements*, Euclid was describing an abstract domain of points and lines that related to a "real world" with only flat surfaces. In 1854, Bernhard Riemann invented a wider theory of mathematics that encompassed both flat (Euclidean) and spherical (non-Euclidean) surfaces. As Bellos stated, "The key concept behind Riemann's theory was the curvature of space. When a surface has zero curvature, it is flat, or Euclidean, and the results of *The Elements* all hold. When a surface has positive or negative curvature, it is curved, or non-Euclidean, and the results of *The Elements* do not hold" (p. 389). Riemann's ideas were counter-intuitive, but they revolutionized both mathematics and physics. His innovations were used by Einstein to formulate his general theory of relativity, which states that the geometry of space-time is not flat but curved.

AC – April 10, 1968

Dogtown (or Dogtown Commons), the location of many Maximus poems, is the site of an abandoned 18th-century settlement covering several acres inland between Rockport and Gloucester, Mass. The area is now a sparsely wooded wasteland containing many haphazardly scattered boulders featuring inscriptions such as INDUSTRY and KEEP OUT OF DEBT carved in the early 20th century.

AC – June 20, 1968

The young New York poet Ed Sanders admired Olson's poetry. Sanders wrote a series of poems about working in a cigar store on Times Square and watching the "Toe Queen" prostitutes in the district. For Sanders' view of this time period, see his book *1968: A History in Verse* (Black Sparrow Press, Santa Rosa, CA, 1997).

CO – June 28, 1968

In Gloucester, the Fiesta is an annual celebration put on by the Sicilian and Italian American community honoring the patron saint of fishermen, St. Peter. It culminates with the Blessing of the Fishing Fleet on the weekend closest to the Feast Day of St. Peter, June 29th.

AC – August 7, 1968

Brother Antoninus was the California poet William Everson, a good friend of Robert Hawley's. The cover of Portents' *Semina* featured a hand-written letter that read,

Dear Sybil,

I wanted to write to you sooner. But I have been busy. I can't come down. I have no way. I have been fine. Do you remember Wiley? Him his sister and Brother Inlay went fishing. Wiley got his hook caught. Dick went out and unhook it. He went down in a hole Jackie went in after him got him by the hair and pulled him in. Just as got him to the bank he said <u>let go</u> she let go and he drowned. Well that's how it goes. Love, Evelyn

CO – August 28, 1968

Inga Lovén was "the lady [who] went back to the continent."

CO – September 14, 1968

The "5th Week" was "from a different series or group"—apparently Olson presented this material in the second part of his two lectures on Alfred North Whitehead at Black Mountain College. I am indebted to the Olson scholar Ralph Maud for this information.

CO – October 11, 1968

Portents never published Olson's "Essay on the Matter Of, for Ann Charters." As he suggested in his previous letter, he was really showing me "the back" of his "mind instead that is of simply laying out the hand as such." Sam and I finally decided, along with Diane di Prima in her East Village little magazine *The Floating Bear,* that Olson, "like Pound, expects you to know his subject as well as he does. Many times [his writing reads] like notes to himself . . ."

AC – November 3, 1968

On October 27, 1968, *The New York Times Book Review* contained a review by M.L. Rosenthal of two Olson books—*Selected Writings of Charles Olson* edited by Robert Creeley (New York: New Directions Press) and *Human Universe and Other Essays* edited by Donald Allen

(New York: Grove Press). Rosenthal praised Olson's writing, quoting from his "Projective Verse" essay as an example of the poet's method of showing "the kind of living action that language is and should be, as opposed to the dead decorum of what we usually think of as beautiful style."

Rosenthal went on to say that Olson was "a sophisticated thinker. He obviously knows his poetic history and is capable of writing passages and whole poems that by most standards have elegance as well as power. He is, in fact, a solid theorist and practitioner in what by this time can well be called the tradition of the experimental." Rosenthal understood that Olson's "playfulness and insistent self-interrupting colloquial emphasis are intended to present a concept of the process of poem-formation at a pitch of involvement that communicates itself actively rather than through conventional exposition. Such exposition, Olson seems to feel, would always be at a remove from the process and would, therefore, falsify it."

Rosenthal especially admired Olson's "Mayan Letters" in Creeley's anthology, in which Olson developed a number of his basic ideas about the neglected values and possibilities inherent in earlier civilizations. The critic understood that Olson's use of historically pertinent documents was similar to the method of William Carlos Williams and Ezra Pound in his role as what Gertrude Stein called "a village explainer." Rosenthal concluded that Olson's continuity with these earlier experimental writers, together with "the energetic, informed engagement of his thinking, and, of course, the exploration of new forward positions in poetry," had been a strong influence on many younger poets.

CO – March 7, 1969

Sirhan Sirhan was the 24-year-old Palestinian immigrant convicted of assassinating Robert F. Kennedy in Los Angeles on June 5, 1968.

CO – June 23, 1969

In 2005, Ralph Maud went through the files relating to "The Special View of History" in the Charles Olson Archive at the Dodd Research Center at UConn. Maud reconstructed specific dates for some of Olson's lectures at Black Mountain College in April and May 1956. Maud also found a sheet in the files that "very probably represents Olson's intentions" for the five lectures he gave later in the fall of 1956 during his two weeks in San Francisco. Olson's outline reads:

The View [of History]

Lecture I, The View

Harrison—Hopi—Tillich

Lecture II, The Process

Lecture III, The Measure (Laws)

Lecture IV, An Example: History 300 BC—1000

Lecture V, Conclusion: Questions

AC – July 8, 1969

On July 6, 1969, the *Boston Sunday Globe* published a review by the staff writer Herbert A. Kenny of three Olson books: *Maximus IV, V, VI; Mayan Letters;* and *Call Me Ishmael: A Study of Melville,* as well as my book *Olson/Melville: A Study in Affinity.* Kenny wrote that "Olson is scholar as well as poet, and when his work is completed we will know New England better for his research and his intuitions. Meanwhile he does not get the critical attention he should. . . ."

Kenny "reviewed" my *Olson/Melville* book in one sentence: "Ann Charters' study is concerned with Olson in relation to Melville, a study of the affinity between them." Then the reviewer concluded that "It is the Maximus poems that are central" to Olson's work, "and they should be brought together in one edition, and made available on the market."

AC – July 24, 1969

The University of California Press published *The Collected Poems of Charles Olson* in 1983, edited by George Butterick; it won that year's American Book Award for editing. I became good friends with George and his wife Colette after I began teaching at the University of Connecticut in Storrs in 1974. The following year, when I was invited by Oxford University Press to write a biography of Olson, I passed the offer on to Butterick. A short time later when George was asked by Gale Research to compile a volume on the group of avant-garde writers associated with the Beats and Black Mountain College for the *Dictionary of Literary Biography* series, he advised them that I could do the job.

George was my closest colleague at UConn. Though a poet himself, he worked tirelessly to clarify Olson's manuscripts and promote his achievement as an important American writer. Butterick died of cancer in 1989, aged 45. In his obituary, the *Los Angeles Times* stated that as Olson's editor, he had "set a standard for scholarly work on contemporary poetry." Butterick took the photograph of me walking with Olson on page 21.

AC – Sept. 29, 1969

The new Portents for which Sam drew the illustrations was Portents 14, "Farther North," a prose piece by Larry Eigner.

Olson Citations Accompanying Photographs

Source: *The Maximus Poems of Charles Olson,* edited by George F. Butterick. Berkeley: University of California Press, 1983.

About Ann Charters

Ann Charters is the author of the first biography of Jack Kerouac, published in 1973, as well as a number of major studies of Beat literature and its personalities. She began taking photographs in 1958 on Andros Island in the Bahamas to document Samuel Charters' field recordings for Folkways Records. These photographs of musicians are featured in *Blues Faces: A Portrait of the Blues* (David Godine Books, 2000). Her photographs of Kerouac, Ginsberg, Kesey, and others are included in *Beats & Company: Portrait of a Literary Generation* (Doubleday, 1986). Her photo essay on Charles Olson in Gloucester was published in *Olson/Melville: A Study in Affinity* (Oyez, 1968). Her photos also illustrated Samuel Charters' *The Poetry of the Blues* (Oak Publications, 1963) and *Songs of Sorrow: Lucy McKim Garrison and "Slave Songs of the United States"* (University Press of Mississippi, 2015). Ann Charters' photo essay featuring the Nobel Prize-winning poet Tomas Tranströmer is included in Samuel Charters' translation of Tranströmer's *Baltics,* published by Tavern Books in 2012.

About Charles Olson

Charles Olson was born in 1910 in Worcester, Massachusetts. His first book, *Call Me Ishmael,* published in 1947, is a case study of Herman Melville's *Moby-Dick.* Olson was an essayist, poet, scholar, and avid letter writer. He was a professor who taught at universities ranging from Clark to Harvard to Black Mountain College. His influence in the 1950s and 1960s was expansive in many fields of thought. He died in New York in 1970 while completing his masterpiece, *The Maximus Poems.*

Tavern Books

Tavern Books is a not-for-profit poetry publisher that exists to print, promote, and preserve works of literary vision, to foster a climate of cultural preservation, and to disseminate books in a way that benefits the reading public.

We publish books in translation from the world's finest poets, new works by innovative writers, and revive out-of-print classics. We keep our titles in print, honoring the cultural contract between publisher and author, as well as between publisher and public. Our catalog, known as The Living Library, sustains the visions of our authors, ensuring their voices are alive in the social and artistic discourse of our modern era.

The Living Library

*forthcoming

Tavern Books is funded, in part, by the generosity of philanthropic organizations, public and private institutions, and individual donors. By supporting Tavern Books and its mission, you enable us to publish the most exciting poets from around the world. To learn more about underwriting Tavern Books titles, please contact us by e-mail: info@tavernbooks.org.

MAJOR FUNDING HAS BEEN PROVIDED BY

Lannan

THE LIBRA FOUNDATION

THE PUBLICATION OF THIS BOOK IS MADE POSSIBLE, IN PART, BY THE SUPPORT OF THE FOLLOWING INDIVIDUALS

Gabriel Boehmer

Dean & Karen Garyet

Mark Swartz & Jennifer Jones

The Mancini Family

Dorianne Laux & Joseph Millar

Pierre Rioux

Mary Ann Ryan

Marjorie Simon

Bill & Leah Stenson

Dan Wieden

Ron & Kathy Wrolstad

Colophon

This book was designed and typeset by Eldon Potter at Bryan Potter Design, Portland, Oregon. The text is set in Garamond, an old-style serif typeface named for the punch-cutter Claude Garamond (c. 1480-1561). Display font Futura was commissioned in 1927 by the Bauer Type Foundry (Frankfurt) and designed by Paul Renner. *Evidence of What Is Said* appears in both paperback and cloth-covered editions. Printed on archival-quality paper by McNaughton & Gunn, Inc.